LEAVE BETTER THAN FOUND

Taylor Jannsen

ISBN: 978-0-9971769-2-6

A sincere and heartfelt thank you to everyone who contributed to this book. To my family, friends, teammates, coaches and players who all played a pivotal role in who I have become, you have influenced me in some way, shape or form. You all have and will continue to leave me better than found.

CONTENTS

INTRODUCTION

"Maybe You Could Write a Book"

The night before I went into surgery for testicular cancer, a young lady whom I have had the pleasure to coach, mentor, and work with for several years sent me this message:

> *"Hey Taylor, I just wanted to let you know that I will definitely be thinking about you the next couple of days, weeks, and months. I can only imagine how tough of a situation this is and what you are all going though right now, but what I have learned from a very great coach is you can never give up and you can always grow from your experiences. I cannot put into words how grateful I am that you are always there to support me no matter the situation. You have not only taught me about basketball, but also about life. There are so many other people that you have influenced and we are all here to support you and fight with you. You are not alone Taylor, and it breaks my heart that such a great person has to go through something like this, but I know that something good will come out of it; maybe you can write a book or something. I know you want nothing to change in the way people treat you, but I just wanted to let you know that I am so appreciative of everything you have done for me, my family, my friends, and the entire community. We love you like family and are praying for the best. I know you can overcome this speed bump, Taylor, and we will be with you every step of the way. You've been my biggest fan and now I get to be yours. Good luck tomorrow! We will be thinking about you."*

Her words managed to shed a tear from my eyes but also to bring me great meaning and joy in the fact that I had been able to make a difference in her life. Being 25 years old, healthy and running a successful business, I never took time to think about what it would be like if I were to be diagnosed with cancer and have to undergo chemotherapy treatment. It's obviously something I would never have wished or planned for, but looking back now, it's a time period for which I am incredibly thankful.

I am now 26 years old, healthy, and continue to run my business, PerformanceMax Basketball Training, LLC, which centers on basketball player development in Southeastern Wisconsin. My time with cancer was a speed bump, just as this young lady stated it would be, but it was also another opportunity for me to grow as a person and gain more perspective in my life.

I officially began my business after my fourth and final year of collegiate basketball in 2011. As a way to connect with players, parents and coaches, I used a monthly newsletter to share information, motivation and stories. I've always loved putting words and thoughts on paper to motivate others, make them feel good, or just make them think. I never envisioned my passion for writing and sharing information to culminate into anything. However, after receiving the message from this young lady, the thought to write a book kept circulating in my mind.

For a few months, I set aside a few hours every week to write. Each time I wrote, I became more driven to produce something of meaning that could positively affect the hearts, minds and actions of anyone willing to listen. The coming pages feature stories, research and strategies that have the ability to help you make positive transformations when applied to your life. Regardless of where you are, who you are, what your circumstances are or what you have done in the past, this book is for you. We each carry substantial worth and importance. In reading this book, my hope is that you will find increased significance, happiness and spread continued positive influence in the lives of others around you. We may not change the world in its entirety, but we each have the ability to entirely change our world and impact the lives of those in it.

Leave Better Than Found (LBTF)

Abbreviations and acronyms are shorter versions of existing words and phrases. They are designed to save time and take up less space when reading something or writing out something. In other words, they are used for simplicity. Often times our lives are anything but simple; we are frequently faced with tough decisions, complex tasks, and varying levels of responsibility. There are multiple ways to accomplish anything, many of which involve a great deal of complexity. In time, however, we often learn the best way is to keep it simple. In searching for a title for this book, I had numerous ideas and thoughts. After drawing out potential title after title, subtitle after subtitle, it finally dawned on me: keep it simple. LBTF, short for Leave Better Than Found, isn't a formula or complicated equation, it is an acronym that is meant to serve as a reminder of the value, potential and capabilities that we each possess.

Where Did This Idea Come From?

I used to say in a whiny tone of voice when I wanted to get out of cleaning something, "It was like this when we got here" or "It was like this before." Like any great parent would say, my mother always patiently replied to me, "It doesn't matter. Leave it better than you found it." As a kid, I would roll my eyes and think, "Why does it matter? No one will notice," or even worse, "Someone else will take care of it."

At the time, I didn't understand why I should take the time and effort to go out of MY way and spend time out of MY day to do more than what was expected. The lesson my mother was teaching me at the time was to be someone who adds value to the world wherever you go and whatever you do. By incorporating the foundations of this book in our everyday lives, we can enrich the lives of others while creating the best version of ourselves. Someday when our time is up, we will leave the world better than we found it.

Foundations of LBTF

The three foundations that make up our ability to "Leave Better Than Found" on both a small, daily scale, as well as a large, lifetime scale, are positive mental attitude (PMA), action, and influence. Each foundation is broken down to give you meaning, understanding and real-life application. Here is a preview of some of the information you will find on the coming pages:

- A positive mental attitude (PMA) isn't just for the person whose life is absent of struggle or frustration.
- Positive mental attitude is for anyone in any circumstance.
- If being happy all the time isn't what positive mental attitude is, then what does it actually mean? How do we adopt it?
- We all have the same amount of time in a day; what do the most successful people in the world do to create long-lasting, sustainable success? Have they really just outworked the rest of the general population, or is there more to it?
- Many people feel that they are in no position to lead, yet we all crave importance. How do we increase significance and meaning in our lives?
- Regardless of position, financial status or past history, we are all in a position to influence others.

Each foundation of LBTF consists of things that both you and I are in 100% control over. Regardless of what has happened, is happening, or what could happen in our lives, we control the foundations of LBTF. NO MATTER WHAT! Your circumstances do not change your ability to have a great attitude, commit to meaningful actions and spread positive influence! You are the driver of the car. You have the ability to leave better than found.

Foundation 1
POSITIVE MENTAL ATTITUDE

Positive mental attitude is not the absence of adversity in our lives. Struggles, setbacks and obstacles will occur. Our only emotion will not be happy-go-lucky; it is natural to feel frustration, sadness, and anger at times and in various situations. A positive mental attitude does mean; however, that we have unconditional gratitude regardless of our circumstances or current life events. It means that even during adverse times we believe there is an opportunity to learn and grow. A positive mental attitude means that we are intentional about our thoughts and words. When we have the choice to pick optimism or pessimism, we choose optimism. Unquestionably, this is not an easy practice; one in which we may never perfect. In our quest to strive for a positive mental attitude, we change the energy around us to someone other people gravitate toward.

CHAPTER 1: PERSPECTIVE

An old Chinese proverb states, "Be careful of your thoughts, for your thoughts become your words. Be careful of your words, for your words become your actions. Be careful of your actions, for your actions become your habits. Be careful of your habits, for your habits become your character. Be careful of your character, for your character becomes your destiny."

What we believe and what we focus our attention on becomes our reality. Do you focus solely on the negative components of your life or do you choose to place your focus on the positive components? In its simplest terms, do you believe life is good or do you believe life sucks? Do you assume people are inherently good or inherently bad? If we naturally believe that the universe is out to get us, and people are inherently bad; we tend to find the bad in our lives and in each person. If we seek the good in our lives, we begin to see just how good our lives are. If we believe that people are genuinely good, we tend to see and bring out the best in those individuals. There is opportunity everywhere to find the good and there is equal opportunity to find the bad; what we look for is what we find.

So many people believe that happiness is a result of what happens to us or what we obtain in our lives. In all actuality, we determine our own happiness by our perspective. I know people who have endless amounts of money, materials and "success" who are miserable. On the flip side, I know people who don't have a lot of money, materials and have been hit with hard circumstances that find something new to be thankful for every day. Why is this? Because these people choose to focus on what's good in the world. What we seek, we find. If we seek the good, we find the good. Our attitude is in our control, a valuable lesson that I was fortunate enough to learn from my mother at a young age.

"It's a Great Day to Be a Duck"

I don't recall our destination or my exact age, but my mom and I were driving. It was pouring down rain outside, and I was full of complaints. My mom finally had enough and turned to me and said, "Ok, now say something positive." Cranky and ornery, I muttered, "It's a great day to be a duck." My mom quickly turned her annoyed emotions to a loud, encouraging "There you go, T." She didn't yell, get mad, or lecture me, but she taught me a lesson I won't ever forget. Whenever one of us is expressing a little too much negativity, we quickly remind the other to keep perspective using, "It's a great day to be a duck." There are always positives in our lives, we just have to search for them!

Along similar lines, I couldn't help but overhear a conversation a while ago between a gentleman and a lady. The lady had just received news that someone in her family was expecting and the child had Down syndrome. She spoke in a very sad, depressing tone. The gentleman, however, spoke in an upbeat, positive tone and explained how he actually knew some families in similar situations. He explained that their children brought them incredible joy and meaning, maybe more so than having a child without Down syndrome. The lady responded by saying something along the lines of "It's just too bad, this is their first child." She would continue to think about and express the potential added stressors to their life and "couldn't imagine" being put in that situation. She clearly heard the gentleman and understood what he was trying to say, but she chose not to seek the perspective that the gentleman was offering. Two similar situations and two completely different perspectives.

It is imperative to understand that what we look for and what we focus our attention on is a choice; grasping this concept is especially crucial in industries such as coaching, teaching and management. Have you ever had a coach, boss or teacher who zapped the energy out of you on a daily basis? We all have experienced this feeling or been in this position. Maybe at times, we are that person to others. Something valuable I have learned as a coach is that there is always an opportunity to focus on positive moments, actions and intentions of players versus turning my attention to only the actions they are doing incorrectly or not to my liking. What I choose to focus on typically determines my attitude towards the players. The attitude I convey has a direct correlation to the energy and effort of my players. Through many experiences, I have found when my attention is focused on negatives, the worse my players' energy becomes, which typically results in decreased performance. I may get a rise in energy from the players temporarily, but exacerbating the negatives consistently never produces sustainable results.

I see numerous people in leadership roles fall into this same trap on a regular basis. Day in and day out they focus their attention only on the negative actions of those they lead. They yell, complain and beg in hopes of getting an increase in urgency and performance. Many don't even realize they are doing it, but each day that goes by, they build an environment in which people do not want to be a part of. They lose their ability to relay a message that actually helps motivate or improve others. They find themselves begging and demanding those they lead to perform certain behaviors. Nobody wants to constantly be yelled at, corrected or told they are wrong. It doesn't inspire them; it does the exact opposite. There will always be times of correction in any leadership position, there has to be. I have found, however, the best leaders can correct and relay information in an uplifting way that doesn't zap the energy out of the room. Positive energy is contagious; negative energy is as well. It all starts with how we focus our attention. Where our attention goes is where energy flows. The more we seek positive behavior, the more we find it.

LBTF:

- Our thoughts and beliefs become a large part of who we become.
- Regardless of our circumstances, there is always opportunity for perspective.
- When we seek the good, we find the good.

CHAPTER 2: THE POWER OF A POSITIVE MENTAL ATTITUDE

My grandpa was diagnosed with type 1 diabetes mellitus when he was just 21 years old. It wasn't until 54 years later at the age of 75 when the disease would start to have its way with him and force amputation of both legs. Prior to the bilateral lower leg amputation, he coined the term "PMA" or "positive mental attitude". He continued to use it throughout and after his surgery. I had never heard the phrase before, but each day that passed my grandpa demonstrated the meaning of a positive mental attitude. I was around him a great deal in the weeks leading up to the surgery, and he never shed a tear and not once did he complain about how life would be following it. Instead, he read, researched, and learned how his life would be after the operation. Whereas many people would have taken some time to feel sorry for themselves, worry and fear; he chose to prepare.

Each step leading up to the surgery and the intensive process afterward, he shocked the doctors with his progress and dazzled them with his mindset. Within four days after major surgery, he was enrolled in one of the most intensive therapy programs in the Milwaukee area. Many people who receive this operation begin the program weeks after the procedure. Today, he is walking, driving and living what most would consider a normal life at his age. I fully believe that the reason why he has continued to overcome diabetes, and now a double leg amputation, is because of his positive mental attitude.

A few months after my grandpa's amputation, I would be forced to face a different type of disease. Luckily for me, I had a role model in my grandpa who showed me how to handle it. On January 2, 2015, I was sitting at home talking to my dad before I went to coach that Friday night. I mentioned to him that I had been having a couple weird symptoms going on with my body. Based on what I told him he told me I needed to go get checked out as quickly as possible (that's saying it nicely as he was a little bit sterner with me about it). I was not and am still not the type of person who asks for help very often; I can be transparent in saying that I am a pretty stubborn individual. Despite my stubborn characteristics, I heeded my father's advice and went to the doctor's office the next morning. Thankfully

I did. I was diagnosed with testicular cancer on the spot. My initial reaction was one of disbelief, like most people's reaction would be. A million things ran through my mind:

- "A lot of people die from cancer."
- "I have a couple more months on my parent's medical insurance, how am I going to afford the bills when I no longer am on their plan?"
- "I'm not going to be able to work during surgery and treatment. My business is going to suffer."
- "I'm not going to be able to attend the upcoming annual vacation with my buddies."

I quickly realized that none of these thoughts were going to help me. I looked for perspective, and I started to find it. My thoughts turned to:

- "I have a form of cancer that is highly treatable; I am young and healthy."
- "I will have access to healthcare that will allow me to get better. Regardless of the expense, nothing is more important than health."
- "The winter is usually a slow time of the year anyway. I can take the time I have off and continue to learn, grow, and improve as a person and as a coach."
- "I have the best group of friends anyone could ask for. They'll understand the situation."

A couple of weeks after my initial diagnosis, I had surgery to remove the cancerous testicle. Many times when men have testicular cancer they undergo surgery, and that's the end of it. In other cases, the cancer spreads to other portions of the body, which then require further surgery or chemotherapy. The doctors waited until after the surgery to take my blood again and to see if they were able to remove all of the cancer or if further treatment would be required. I received the news a few days after surgery that the cancer had spread, and I would undergo, in the doctor's words, "a strong dosage of chemotherapy for nine weeks." The doctors explained the physical effects it would have on my body. Symptoms such as fatigue, nausea, suppressed appetite, amongst others were all common. Admittedly, I felt all the effects in some manner at some point during my treatments. I had a couple of days where I couldn't keep food down. My body often times felt weak, but I knew I had a choice each day of what my attitude was going to be. My mind would carry me through what my body could not.

Throughout my treatments, I maintained a fairly regular work schedule, worked out three times a week and lived as normally as I could. When people asked how I was feeling, no matter what, I always told them "I am doing great!" Even though there were times I felt anything but great, I chose to keep my attention off those feelings and instead focus my energy on feeling as good as I possibly could. To some, it sounds ridiculous, but with a positive mental attitude I know I was able to limit the side effects and complications of my chemotherapy just as my grandpa was able to do following his amputations. There is real power in positive mental attitude.

LBTF:

- The storms in our life are inevitable, unfortunate things do happen.
- We always have a choice on how we respond to the circumstances we are faced with.
- There is power in choosing a positive mental attitude as opposed to a negative mental attitude.

CHAPTER 3: ENERGY GIVERS VS. ENERGY TAKERS

Are there people in your life that automatically liberate you with their presence? Are there others that do the exact opposite; that make you feel small or drain your enthusiasm with negativity? What are some of the qualities of the people that give you energy? On the contrary, what are some of the qualities of the people who drain you of your energy?

During my collegiate basketball career, our coach frequently asked us in team meetings if we were giving energy to the team or taking energy from the team. He ultimately was asking us to reflect on our attitude each day. Was our attitude increasing or decreasing the energy in the locker room, in the film room and on the practice floor? Coach always told us that if each person strived to be an energy giver that collectively we could always pick each other up during times of struggle or on days when certain individuals weren't at their best. He also knew the negative effect that could result when a team was full of energy takers. A team full of energy takers would crush enthusiasm, decrease morale and bring others down rather than lift them up. Here are some qualities that make up energy givers and energy takers.

Energy Givers

- Believe their lives are generally good.
- No matter the obstacles they are presented with, they are able to keep a positive mental attitude and maintain enthusiasm.
- Focus their attention on solutions, rather than mindless complaints.
- Encourage others to follow their dreams, visions, and aspirations.
- Lift the spirits of others.
- See failure as an opportunity to learn and grow.
- See the world from a perspective of optimism. "The best is yet to come."

Energy Takers

- Believe life is miserable and are never able to "catch a break."
- There is always something going wrong in their life.
- Constantly complain without seeking a solution.

- Discourage other people's dreams, visions, and aspirations.
- Love to criticize and condemn.
- See failure as permanent or a result of their "bad luck".
- See the world from a perspective of pessimism, "It's only going to get worse."

Based on the qualities listed above, are you an energy giver or an energy taker? If you aren't adding energy to the room, what are you doing to take it away? This is a difficult question and takes a lot of humility to answer. If you're compelled to do so, seek out the opinions of people who love you and are close to you. Recognize that they have good intentions in their critiques. How can you start to transform yourself from a person that no one wants to be around to a person that people enjoy being around?

Dealing with Energy Takers

I believe in positive energy. The research is plentiful about the benefit of optimism as opposed to pessimism; positivity creates positive results, as well as longer, healthier lives. The research, however, is not why I believe in positive energy. I have seen the effects in my own life as well as the lives of others that proves the power of positivity. The critics and cynics will call success blind luck or blame their own circumstances as to why they are unable to achieve something. Unquestionably and unfortunately, our world has a plethora of negative energy. Many people have given up on their dream; some just are not willing to work toward theirs. Other individuals have made the conscious choice to be miserable. Often times being around these types of people, or "energy takers" can bring out negative energy within ourselves.

How do we overcome this? The easiest way is to remove that negative energy from your life. Surround yourself with optimists; people who are constantly looking and seeking the good in their lives. Research has shown that we become a combination of the five people we spend the most time with. If you are surrounded constantly by negative people, either they need to change or you need to make a change! The choice is yours, but understand that people will only change when THEY are ready to change. Don't focus too much time and energy on seeing the potential in someone, when they are not making efforts on their end.

In some situations, understandably, you may not be able to remove a person from your life. Maybe it's a boss, teammate or colleague. Whatever the case is, we must understand that our own positive energy must always be stronger than our negative energy. Positive energy is like a muscle, the more we train it, the stronger it gets. The stronger our positive energy, like a muscle, the more ability that we have to overcome outside forces, such as the negative mental attitudes of others. Positive energy is also contagious, the more we tap into it, the more it spreads.

The 80-20 Rule

Lou Holtz, a former NCAA Division 1 football coach, put it brilliantly: "80% of people you complain to don't care, and 20% are glad you have problems." I love this quote. I will preface this by saying that complaining is talking negatively about a person, place or situation for no other reason than just to complain. It's mindless; it is simply talking and complaining because we feel better about ourselves when we do it or we have nothing positive that we would like to focus on. No one cares about the type of complaining that Lou Holtz is addressing. Everyone has problems they face; we all have people we don't get along with, and we all are placed in situations at some point that are less than ideal. The problem with mindless complaining is that it provides no solutions.

"My coach sucks." This is a phrase that is becoming used way too often in youth sports. Admittedly, some coaches are not very good, but when the first thing out of a player's or parent's mouth in explaining lackluster perfomance is something that attacks or questions the coach, I immediately take anything else they say with a grain of salt. Blaming someone else is one of the easiest things to do in various parts of our lives. When something isn't going our way, there is tendency to look everywhere besides the mirror.

Recently, a young player tried out for a team that I coach and talked about how he was mistreated. He blamed the previous season going poorly because of the coach. The kid said something to the effect that the plays they ran didn't work and the coach didn't know how to substitute. Any chance he did have of making our roster went up in flames after hearing him speak in that light. I don't know whether his coach sucked or not, that's not the point. The point is that this player chose to inform me (a coach) about his previous school season by telling me about how his coach was the reason behind his lackluster performance. Regardless of the validity to his story, the last type of kid that I want on my team is someone that immediately looks for someone else to blame.

It's easy to point the finger at someone else, make excuses and complain. It's hard to accept responsibility, find solutions, and do everything in your power to make the best of the circumstances you have. You may not like your coach, boss or teammate. There is a chance it might not be all your fault, but things are only going to get worse if you rationalize your underperformance by making excuses, complaints and finger-pointing. If we are going to take the time to find the negative in people, places or situations, then we better take double the time to offer and present a solution.

LBTF:

- Focus on being an energy giver. Wherever you go, whatever you do, be someone who raises the energy of the room.
- Surround yourself with energy givers.
- Avoid mindless complaining. If you have a complaint, work twice as hard to find a solution.

CHAPTER 4: CONFLICT

It is nearly impossible for everyone to be completely happy with the decisions we make in every situation. I will never forget an email I received as a coach at the end of a basketball season. We had just lost a pivotal game to advance to a Sweet 16 game of an extremely large and talented field of teams. We played nothing close to our best. What made the game worse is that while we still found a way to have a lead toward the end of the game. We eventually lost on a game-winning shot at the buzzer. I had a flurry of emotions following the game ranging from upset, disappointed and helpless.

Within minutes after the conclusion of the game, a parent sent an email to myself and all of the other parents that stated something along the lines of, "At least we can take away one positive thing from this loss; that my kid had NOTHING to do with it." The comment was meant to be a jab at me, and it stemmed from her son not receiving a great deal of playing time. When we selected our group for this team, I based the decision on players' potential, character and how good of a teammate he would be. This particular player was and is a great kid. On more than one occasion, I picked him up for practices and games, often driving a great distance out of the way to do so. I believed in him and cared about him as I do every player. He, like others, when given his opportunity (granted it was a small opportunity) didn't play well that game. I didn't coach well.

So as any coach can imagine, when I received this email, I nearly lost it. I played back the kids' mistakes in my head, the poor performances he had at recent practices and the times I went out of my way to help this family out. I had heard rumblings of complaints and criticisms from this parent throughout the year already so I was on the edge of losing it. I drafted up an email to "stick it" to this parent.

Then I stopped, took a deep breath, and erased the whole email. I didn't respond. I thought about five things that I really liked about the kid. After all, he wasn't the one whom I had the problem with. Not once did

HE complain about his situation. While I can be honest in saying he wasn't a great player, he always worked hard each and every practice and certainly gave his best effort in each game. Lashing back at this parent would only hurt the kid and wouldn't prove anything to anyone. The temporary feeling of power that I would feel by unleashing my anger through this email would quickly dissolve and probably lead to an ongoing dispute from which no one would have gained clarity, only frustration. My positive energy needed to be stronger than my negative energy. My positivity needed to be strong enough to overcome her negativity.

A couple of days later, she emailed me stating that her son would not be participating in our last tournament of the season. I emailed her back thanking her son for his commitment along with two specific and sincere compliments about him as a person. Through my past experiences, I was able to activate my positive muscle and overcome the negative forces that I was faced with. It wasn't easy to handle the situation in this manner, but I now look back and am happy with how I handled it.

Conflict Resolution

Admittedly, a few years ago I wouldn't have handled the aforementioned situation in the same manner. I always tried to get the last word, was quick to react and would let my emotions from previous conflicts carry over for days, weeks and sometimes months. Whether it was a conflict with a girlfriend, family member, friend, a player's parent, or another player, I certainly haven't always resolved conflicts in a positive manner. While I am nowhere near perfect to this day, I have tried to learn from past situations to help me in similar scenarios down the road. Here are some tips and a few things I have learned that hopefully can help you better resolve conflict with people in your life.

1.) 24-Hour Rule

I use this with every team that I coach and find it applicable to other parts of our lives. Players and parents must wait 24 hours after a game or practice to contact me about an issue involving playing time or something they are upset with. So often, we are most vulnerable to lashing out immediately and reacting in a manner that is only detrimental to ourselves, the other person or any other person involved in a conflict. Typically, when we lash out, so does the other person. When two people are in an argument full of reactions, not much good typically comes out of it. When we allow buffering time to wait, collect ourselves, and handle the conflict in a mature, professional way, it often turns out better. We won't always reach a perfect conclusion, but we often can gain more clarity and understanding moving forward.

2.) No Emails

This can be tough in this day and age, but I believe using email to alleviate conflict can be a very dangerous and often times slippery slope. We are often left with interpreting the other person's tone and angle, which in many cases our interpretation could be completely wrong. Instead of emailing, ask to set up a call or meet in person. If email is your only outlet for response, write your first draft out. Read it over. Take a deep breath and erase it. Write it over. I have found that when drafting an email we often don't even realize that we can come across as negative, condescending and critical without even meaning to. When we read it back to ourselves, we often have a better feel for the tone of our message and can continue on writing something that comes across in a better manner.

3.) Vent to Someone

Find someone outside of your immediate situation with whom you can talk. A lot of times when we talk to someone else we find out what we are upset with or what we are stressing about is minor. In other instances, the person we talk to often has an idea that can contribute to positively resolving the conflict.

4.) Exercise

Whenever I need to clear my mind, I always resort to some form of exercise. Exercise releases endorphins, which improve mood. Sometimes all we need is a refreshed mind and a better mood to gain control over our emotions and the handling of a conflict.

5.) Deep Breaths

Slowing down our breaths and becoming aware of our thoughts can help us eliminate wasted energy on things that don't matter. Deep breaths soothe and relax us. Being in a more relaxed state while addressing a situation helps avoid knee-jerk reactions that are filled with anger.

6.) Be Intentional with Your Words

This is really important and can change the tone of an entire conversation. Starting a sentence with "you" often sends a message that we are attacking that person, which automatically puts them on the defensive. For example, if someone were to say, "You need to communicate with me more," we all would be more defensive than if someone said, "We need to communicate more." Keeping the conversation non-biased and from a non-attacking vantage point changes the way people respond to what you are saying.

LBTF:

- Conflict is a part of life, how we handle the conflicts in our lives is crucial in building relationships and shaping future endeavors.
- Your positive energy must be stronger than your negative energy; your positivity must be stronger than another person's negativity.
- Use the six ideas given in conflict resolution to better handle the conflicts that come up in your life.

CHAPTER 5: LINGUISTIC INTENTIONALITY

How many times have you said this before, "I have to work" or "I have to go to school," or maybe "I have to go to practice"? What if we instead replaced the word "have" with "get" in each of those sentences? A change in one word can automatically change our feelings from obligated or burdened, to feelings of gratitude and opportunity.

- We get to go to work because we are fortunate enough to have a job.
- We get to go to school because we are fortunate enough to receive an education.
- We get to go to practice because we are fortunate enough to be a part of a team.

For most, we could go even deeper:

- We get to work and attend school because we live in a country with a prosperous economy as well as an education system.
- We get to compete in athletics because we have a body that is healthy enough to be able to do so.

Technically, none of us "have" to do anything. We have a choice of action each day. Rather than putting ourselves into feelings of obligation, we can change our feelings to one of opportunity!

"I'm Okay"

"I'm okay" or "I'm fine" are common responses when people ask others how they are doing. I always struggle to understand those responses. Most people reading this book probably live in the United States of America, in which there is access to education, clean drinking water, an abundance of food, and personal freedom. When we tell ourselves that we are "okay" or "fine" we act in a way that someone doing "okay" or "fine" behaves. When we tell ourselves that we are "great", "terrific" or "really well", we have a tendency to behave in that way as well. Some of you may be thinking "I don't want to be fake." My argument would be to speak in terms of the person you want to become, not the person you are or think you are right now.

Your perception is your reality. Merely changing your language isn't a guarantee you will become great, you need to truly start believing and carrying it out in your actions. If you keep saying you're "okay" or "fine", then you will keep living a life that is just okay or fine. Maybe that's fine by you, but it's not okay for me!

LBTF:

- A simple shift in our word choices can play a huge part in transforming the way we think and feel.
- Choose "get to" instead of "have to" in everything you do.
- When someone asks how you are, respond in the manner of the person you would like to become.

CHAPTER 6: THE GROWTH MINDSET

To bridge the gap between who we are today and who we want to become, there first needs to be a shift in how we think. To get closer to our true potential, this shift needs to be that who we become is not dependent on our circumstances.

The growth mindset states that our talents and abilities can be developed through effort, practice and persistence. The fixed mindset is one in which we believe that our talents and abilities are given to us or we are "born with them". People with a growth mindset are typically able to respond to failure or challenges in their life better than those with a fixed mindset. If we believe that our talents are fixed or inborn, then we will avoid failure and challenges at all costs because failure is a reflection of our competence. If we believe that our abilities can grow with persistence and effort, then we seek challenges and take failure as an opportunity to learn and improve.

Famous author, John Maxwell, wrote an entire book titled, "Sometimes You Win, Sometimes You Learn." Every opportunity or event in our lives is one from which we can seek personal growth if we choose to look at it from the right perspective. The person who believes that our talents and abilities can be shaped by things within our control has the opportunity for true personal growth. On the flip side, the person who believes that we are what we are and have no ability to learn and grow will struggle to maximize their individual potential.

Adversity as a Catalyst for Success

Adversity in our lives can often be the catalyst for our biggest triumphs or accomplishments. In any circumstance, positive or negative, there is always opportunity to learn and grow. Michael Jordan was once cut from his varsity basketball team as a sophomore in high school and later became the best male basketball player in the history of the sport. Jim Carey was a high school drop-out at the age of 15 when he became a janitor to help support his struggling family; he has since went on to be the star in several of the highest-grossing comedy films ever produced. Jay-Z went from a single-parent household in the projects of Brooklyn, New York, to one of the greatest artists of our generation. JK Rowling was once jobless, divorced, and a single mother of a young child and later was able to sell more than 400 million copies of her Harry Potter books. Each faced different types of struggles, but the commonality between all of them was that they never let their struggles remain permanent.

I especially enjoyed reading about Rowling's story. Rowling graduated from college in 1986 and, seven years later, she found herself divorced with an infant daughter. She moved to a different country with her daughter to be closer to her sister. She brought with her three chapters of a book that would later become Harry Potter. After her move, she battled clinical depression, contemplated suicide, and signed up for welfare benefits. During this time, she also says she turned her focus to writing. In 1995, she finished the first Harry Potter manuscript which ended up being rejected by 12 major publishers. A year later, a small publishing house accepted it and gave her a small advance. In 1997, one thousand copies of her book were published, 500 of which were distributed to libraries. These are extremely small quantities in the publishing world, but as people began to catch wind of the story, demand for the book increased. Over time, Rowling began to experience a level of success that would soon make her regarded as one of the best-selling authors of all time. Rowling openly says that the hardest time in her life was also the catalyst for her success.

I know a turning point in my young life was when I was cut from an AAU basketball program in the summer of my 8th grade season. Not making the team crushed me. Finding out my friend made the team and I didn't crushed me even more. Without that experience in my life, however, I wouldn't be the coach I am today and would most likely never have had the opportunity to play collegiate basketball. I was never a kid who slacked off or gave minimal effort, but that moment sparked a whole new work ethic I never had before. I woke up early to work on my game before school, I went to practice early and stayed late, sometimes hours at a time (much to the exhaustion of a couple of my coaches). I was always looking for an edge to improve.

That same passion still exists in me today in working with players. A moment in my life that was devastating at the time was actually a catalyst for many of my future accomplishments. No one asks for adversity, but the reality is that there will always be adversity in our lives. We have to be able to find the underlying value in our experiences. For me, I found out that I wasn't good enough, and that in order to become good enough I'd have to work harder than everybody else did. Struggles and adversity in our lives are not permanent unless we let them be. Sometimes we won't understand why certain things happen, but there is always a message in each of our experiences. Persist in the face of your struggles, and you will undoubtedly come out better for having had those experiences.

Practice

People often think of a productive practice or training session as the flawless execution of drills or exercises. The truth of the matter is that a perfect practice does not make perfect. Real learning takes place in a practice environment in which we are performing activities that force us out of our comfort zone. There should be times in which we fail or struggle; these are the times in which we make corrections and can acquire new skill or knowledge. We must be willing to shift our mindset from avoiding mistakes to aiming for mistakes. This isn't to say that we should purposely start making mistakes, or that we make them out of laziness or mindless activity. Mistakes within our practice and learning environments should be made because we are pushing ourselves to the edge of our capabilities. We have to accept being challenged, and be willing to make mistakes. When we adopt the willingness to do so, we unlock unlimited potential for personal growth.

When I run a basketball camp or clinic, it's interesting to observe the players who seek out and embrace challenges as opposed to avoiding them. An example would be the kid who jumps to the front of line to demonstrate a drill after I have explained it as opposed to the kid who moves to the back of the line in fear of making a mistake. Another example would be a kid who seeks out the best player in the gym to compete with in a one-on-one drill. Most times that kid who sought the challenge gets beat, sometimes crushed, but that tells me about the player. I know he or she is going to continue to get better. I often remind players that if they are coming to the gym seeking perfection, they're in the wrong place. There is an old expression that if you are the best player at your playground, you need to find a new playground. It has the same meaning in our lives. Seek challenges. Accept them as a means to learn and grow. Get comfortable being uncomfortable.

LBTF:

- A growth mindset means that we believe our abilities can be developed through effort, practice and persistence.

- We don't necessarily wish for adverse times in our lives, yet with a growth mindset, we can take adversity or failure and use it as a catalyst for future success.

- Get comfortable being uncomfortable to maximize your personal growth. For example, read things that make you think, adopt a new exercise program, or pursue new, challenging opportunities within your job when they are presented.

CHAPTER 7: GRATITUDE

Cultivate an attitude of gratitude in your life. Chances are, if you are reading this book, you have an infinite amount for which to be grateful. However, so many people I encounter on a daily basis choose to talk about the things they don't have or complain about people, systems and things that aren't fair. Take a second to stop reading and just look around. Chances are that you have access to shelter, drinking water, clothes and food. Continue looking. You probably have a car, television, couch, oven and a bed. We oftentimes neglect the simple fact that we did nothing to deserve any of these things besides being born in the United States. There are so many people in the world that can only dream of sitting on a couch with a bowl of popcorn and watching a movie. It's easy to get caught up in things we don't have or wishing we had more.

An artist by the name of J-Cole released a song titled "Love Yourz" in 2014. The lyrics speak to listeners about gratitude, and they resonated deeply with me. The chorus goes, "No such thing as a life that's better than yours." He goes on later in the song to talk about how there will always be clothes, cars and houses that might be better than the ones we have, but we are never happy until we love what we have first. He talks about money being worthless without happiness and the beauty of hard times with the people you love. Every situation in your life, good or bad, there is opportunity to be grateful. Even with everything going on in your life, there is always someone else out there wishing for what you have.

For everything you wish you had, identify three things you do have for which you can be grateful. See how your perception of what you have and the world around you changes. I use a strategy to cultivate an "attitude of gratitude" each morning as I eat my breakfast by writing three specific things for which I am especially grateful. Those things often range from my family, friends, and parts of my profession, to the place I live and the car I drive. It's a powerful strategy and I have found it to be a great way to start the day. No longer am I starting my day thinking about the stress, worries or fears in my life; instead, I start each day thinking about the things for which I am grateful.

Thanksgiving

Most families gather on the fourth Thursday in November to eat a hearty meal, watch football, and enjoy each other's company. More importantly, families gather to take time to express gratitude and appreciation for the good in their lives before they begin their meal. How many of us practice a similar routine all the time?

- Why can't the norms of Thanksgiving become a part of our daily lives?
- Would you agree that if we intentionally focused on all that is good in our lives each day that we would feel fuller with appreciation and gratitude?
- Would you agree that we would spend less time complaining?

A great exercise is performing a gratitude prayer before each meal. Name three things for which you are feeling thankful!

Tell Them You Love 'Em

This is extremely powerful. I ran across a passage on Twitter in loving memory of the victims lost in the 9/11 terrorist attacks. The words strike a deep chord about being grateful and living your life with appreciation for the things you have and the people to whom you are closest.

> *"At this moment 13 years ago, millions of Americans went to bed quietly, with no thought that the next morning their world would change forever. That night, hundreds packed flight bags they would not live to open. Thousands slept with loved ones for the last time. One never knows what a new day has in store. Let us live each day to the fullest, and never miss a chance to let those dearest to us know of our love for them. So TONIGHT if you have someone in your life that you love, tell them."*

We live in a world in which it is very easy and efficient to communicate with other people regardless of distance apart. Have you ever received a text message or an email from someone that made your day? We can do the same thing for others. It doesn't need to be lengthy or take an inordinate amount of time, it just needs to be thoughtful.

If you are married, do you think if you actively looked for and sought one thing that you loved and appreciated about your significant other each day and expressed it to them that your relationship would be stronger? If you are a boss or a coach do you think if at the end of each day you complimented a player or employee on a job well done that you would increase organizational morale?

Heartfelt Letters

When I look back on graduation gifts, birthday presents or other unique days in my life, for the most part I don't remember the material gifts, amount of money, or what I bought with a gift card. What I do remember, and still hold onto, are heartfelt letters given to me by others. For my high school graduation, my mother, one of my friends, and my high school basketball coaches each wrote me hand-written letters that I still have to this day.

During my time with cancer, I received overwhelming support in the form of texts, calls, visits, emails, and notes. Nothing was more powerful than the notes I received from players with whom I was currently working or had worked with in the past. During this time, I realized the impact I was making on others. A hardship in my life helped me to realize the difference I was making; it reaffirmed the reason why I do the things I do. For that, I am extremely grateful.

Today, rather than having paintings, posters or images plastered all over my walls, I have notes written by players (some notes from my time with cancer, others from previous seasons) hung up to remind me of why I do what I do.

Sometimes we all wake up a little sleepy or unmotivated. All I need is to look toward the notes hung up on my walls, and it's easy to remember my purpose. Here are a couple of notes I have hung up. This one is from a young man with whom I coached for several years and built a special relationship with his family:

> *"Don't give up. Don't ever give up. First of all, I would like to thank you for everything you've done for me. Whether it be something you've taught me in*

the gym or insight on life and how to be successful. I truly am thankful to call you my coach, role model, and most importantly, family. I know you can beat this because you are the one who taught me about strength and perseverance, so I know you are filled with it."

Another is from a young kid who attends many of my camps and clinics. I copied the note in the form that it was given to me so there are obviously spelling and grammar mistakes, which means even more knowing that the kid wrote it on his own without a parent telling him what he was supposed to say or do.

"I have been thinking about you. If I was lazy in those workouts you have been there and got me better. You are the only coach that I know that wants me to get every little detail and help me reach my full potentials. I always improve my skills even if it is the littlest thing. I started attacking the rim because those workouts. I was always scared of attacking the rim. I hope you will be my coach one day. I hope you feel better."

I truly savored the words of not only these letters, but the numerous other notes I received from players, parents and coaches. I am not saying that in a world full of advanced technology that we need to hand-write everything, but, when given the opportunity, we should all get out a pen, paper, and write someone a heartfelt letter. They will appreciate it, remember it and savor it.

LBTF:

- Cultivate an attitude of gratitude in your life. Start by writing three things each morning that you are grateful for or state three things that you are grateful for before a meal.
- Take time to show appreciation and thanks for all the small and big things in your life.

- Our time on earth is short, tell the people closest to you how much you love, appreciate and value them.
- Hand-written, heartfelt letters are always the strongest way to show your gratitude toward someone else.

FOUNDATION 2
ACTION

How do we bridge the gap between who we are today and who we wish to become? First, we must understand who it is we want to become and the direction we want our lives to take. We then can prioritize what's truly important and focus on specific activities that will help us get closer to who we want to become. Whether it be short-term or long-term, we all have aspirations and things that we want to accomplish. Our ability to turn an aspiration into a reality hinges on the actions we choose to take or choose not to take. In other words, the gap between where we are now and where we want to go is largely based on what we choose to do.

Aspirations without commitment, will remain aspirations. Wanting something or setting a goal to achieve something isn't enough. Often times we want things to come easy. We crave the end-result, but not the grind. We want the fortune, but we don't want to do the things it takes to receive it.

People who have achieved success in anything didn't get to that level by coincidence or by merely wanting something. There are certain things they do that allow them to separate themselves from the crowd. Each of us has the ability to bridge the gap of who we are today and who we want to become, but we must be willing to take the actions necessary in order to do so. Your path will often times be anything but smooth, but in taking action to become who you want to be, you positively impact your own life as well as the lives of those around you.

CHAPTER 8: VISION

Before you begin to take action, it is extremely important to clarify the vision for your life. Your vision is deeper than a list of goals. It's your sense of purpose. It comes from a place in your heart. It involves things that are most important to you and the impact you want to have on the world. For example, a teacher's vision might be to transform the hearts and mold the minds of as many young people as possible. For a mother, it may be to create an environment that allows her children happiness, safety and belonging. As time goes on, your vision may evolve, and your priorities may change, but in bringing clarity to your vision you have a sense of who you want to become. Action without an idea of who you are and who you would like to become often leads to unfocused, unproductive usage of your time.

When you understand who you want to become, you can then can immerse yourself in the process of becoming the person you want to be. That process doesn't involve setting goals, it involves making commitments. People often think they are raising the bar for themselves by creating a list of goals, but in all actuality they are limiting themselves. Higher than any goal you set is a daily commitment to your attitude, action, and influence. Each item is completely within your control.

In its preliminary stages, your vision may start out as simple as, "I want to be someone who helps others." It may be something more specific and complex such as, "I want to be the best athlete, mother, father, engineer, coach, or nurse I possibly can be." No one can tell you who you want to become; I will only help give you strategies on how to get there once you have a vision for your life. I have listed three simple questions that you can ask yourself to help bring clarity to your vision. I highly encourage you to write these questions down and spend time in answering them.

1.) What are the most important things in your life? These could be things such as money, health, social life, service, work, family, status, recognition, respect, and education. Identify the three things that you value the most. This may be difficult to identify only three, but it is important to prioritize your life based on what is most important to you. This doesn't mean that you engage in only three activities every day of your life, it means that you understand which things are the biggest priorities in your life.

2.) What are five personality characteristics that you most value? Traits such as sense of humor, caring, sympathetic, loyal, honest, passionate, and humble are a few examples. Again, it may be difficult to identify only five, and it doesn't mean that other traits are not important, but in clarifying your vision, it is important to identify what personal traits you most value.

3.) How do you want to be remembered? Someday when your time is up, what do you want your legacy to be? What do you want to be the most proud of looking back on your life? What things would give you the greatest sense of fulfillment?

Having an understanding of who you want to become will help direct the decisions you make on a daily basis. It might mean that you need to cut certain things out of your life that don't align with your vision. For example, if being the best athlete you can be is important to you, drinking and partying should not be part of your frequent activities. It may also mean that there are things you need to invest more time in to bridge the gap of where you are now and who you want to become. Using the same example, if you want to become the best athlete in which you can be, it will probably mean that you will need to spend time outside of practice training your mind and body. Whatever it may be, you are responsible for your actions. Having a clear vision will allow you to align your actions and direct your energy, attention and focus to what is truly important in your life.

Shift Your Focus

In our results-oriented world, an often used strategy is to set goals with an end point and a quantifiable result. We all probably know someone in our life who wants to lose a set number of pounds by a given date. Most businesses have revenue goals that they strive to achieve every quarter. I work with several kids that have a goal to receive an athletic scholarship. Most people set these type of goals to direct focus towards something that is desirable or deemed important. Those who set goals feel as though it will be a motivating factor or driving force in the achievement of a specific outcome.

Much more valuable than a list of goals, however, is a list of commitments. How do we actually bridge the gap between where we are today and where we want to be? We bridge the gap by our commitments to controllable actions on a daily basis; immersing ourselves in a process to become our personal best. There is no goal that we can set that has a higher ceiling than if each day we commit to our personal best. Like John Wooden, the former legendary UCLA Men's Basketball Coach, once said, "I've yet to meet a cynic who can describe for me what you can do beyond one's best."

Too often we put numbers and benchmarks on success and then determine our value based on the outcome of certain goals. The problem with that is that we don't always have control over a given number or benchmark. For example, a team whose goal is to win a championship doesn't have full control over injuries, officials and opponents. A business doesn't have complete control over a buyer's decision. There are only certain elements within each party's control; those controllable items are where their attention needs to go.

When we focus on controlling the controllable (attitude, action and influence), we release ourselves from external pressures and the self-imposed stress of achieving a quantifiable result; we first have to be willing to cleanse ourselves from the outcome-based goals we too often set. There will be times in which we fail, struggle and face adversity, this is part of the process.

As I discussed before, in each experience of our lives, there is always opportunity to learn and grow. Our worst experiences can often be a catalyst for our future success. In letting go of outcomes, and committing to be our personal best, we can direct all of our energy to things within our control. As we commit to the process of pursuing daily excellence we also come to find that outcomes are not suppressed, they are actually increased.

PerformanceMax Basketball Training, LLC

A question I am frequently asked as a business owner is, "What's the goal of your business?" I usually respond with, "To help as many players as I can and to be the best coach I can be." Most people respond with a look of confusion and then say, "No, I mean like do you want to open a facility, coach in college, like what's your real goal?" I respond back and say, "I really don't know. I have never put much thought into it. I have always felt as if I commit to helping people and being the best I can be, the right opportunities will continue to present themselves." My vision is controllable; it's not number or status-driven. I have control over my influence on players by my actions and my attitude towards them.

When I started my business in 2011, I didn't have a business plan and didn't make any projections of what I wanted to make. What I did do was commit to staying up late and waking up early every day to be the best coach I could be. I treated every client like they were my only client. I was enthusiastic, energetic and passionate every time I walked onto the court no matter how tired I was. Starting out, I offered my services to local communities for free to increase the exposure I was getting. I wanted to begin building relationships that could eventually lead to increased opportunity in the future. I made a commitment to the process. Did I want to make money right away? Of course. It wasn't my driving force. I can say with certainty that if my goal would have been solely to make a given amount of money or to open a facility at a certain date, I would not be where I am today. The vision I had for my life was much bigger than money. I wanted to make an impact. I had a vision to touch as many players' lives through the game of basketball as I possibly could. That vision remains true today as does my continued commitment to the process of being my personal best. As a result, I have worked with thousands of athletes from multiple states and have increased revenue each year I've been in business. You don't have to have a list of quantifiable goals to be successful, but you do have to have a clear vision of who you want to become and a willingness to commit to the daily process it takes to get there.

LBTF:

- Clarify your vision to better align your behaviors with your aspirations.
- Worry less about goals, and more about commitments.
- There is no higher standard or goal than committing to your vision, and immersing yourself in being your personal best. In doing so, outcomes are not suppressed, but enhanced.

CHAPTER 9: ACCEPTANCE OF DISCIPLINE

My grandpa's other famous acronym during his leg amputation was "AOD" or "acceptance of discipline". Just like positive mental attitude, it is a phrase that he uses to help him lead his life. As I sat with him in the hospital five days after his leg amputations, he was in great spirits and unfazed by his new challenges. A part of me actually thinks he was enjoying maneuvering his wheelchair through tight spots and learning new ways to perform his activities of daily living.

As we sat and talked, one of his doctors came in to take his blood and check up on him. Like usual, his blood was already taken and recorded. The doctor looked at him and she smiled. He shrugged his shoulders and said, "What?" The doctor replied, "It is impressive how you are always on top of your game." Grandpa said, "It's just AOD, I have been doing it my whole life." I looked at him, not sure what he meant. He knew what I was thinking, so he simply said "acceptance of discipline." I sat back in my chair, my mind spinning, and just thought, "Wow." Like "PMA" I had never heard him use that phrase before, but it was clear that his life had been guided by each of these acronyms.

Acceptance of discipline means things that need to be done in our lives are done when they need to be done, how they need to be done, and regardless of if we want to do them. Before his amputations, my grandpa lived with minimal diabetic complications for 54 years. That's not a coincidence. He checks his blood constantly and is always proactive with his health. After the surgery, he was able to accelerate the recovery process because when his doctors told him to do something, whether he felt like it or not, he did it. He accepted and still accepts discipline in his life.

Principles vs. Feelings

Eric Thomas, a motivational speaker, says, "Behind every principle is a promise, behind every feeling is nothing." Thomas is telling us to live by our principles, not our feelings. Feelings are tied to our current state of emotion. When we act on our feelings it often times goes against our core vision and can be paralyzing in the quest of becoming the person we want to be. When we live by our principles we make a commitment and a decision to strive towards personal excellence. Here are a few examples:

- We might FEEL like complaining, but we live by our principle of practicing gratitude regardless of our circumstances.
- We might FEEL like yelling at a player, coworker or child but we live by our principle of encouragement.
- We may not FEEL like working out at 6 AM, but instead of sleeping in, we live by our principle of exercising on a consistent basis.
- We may not FEEL like pursuing our dreams, but we live by the principle of faith and go after our dreams, rather than letting the feeling of fear push us away from our aspirations.

We can quickly begin to see that each moment we are guided by our feelings, we negate our efforts to become our best. Days turn into weeks and, before we know it, we are unhappy with the life we have made for ourselves. The people who are successful in their craft (i.e., athletes, parents, teachers, executives, etc.) are more often than not successful for a reason. They are guided by day to day principles, not paralyzed by feelings!

Living each day by principles is a promise to yourself to commit to being the best you can become. You will hit road blocks, and there will plenty of days you FEEL less than ideal, but you will also begin to set new marks for yourself that you may have never thought were possible.

LBTF:

- Accept discipline into your life.
- Do the things that need to be done, when they need to be done, how they need to be done, regardless if you want to do them.
- Live by principles, not feelings.

CHAPTER 10: THE COMPOUND EFFECT

Why do people in our country struggle with weight loss? Many people desire to lose weight, but end up unsuccessful. Others lose a lot of weight, but then are unable to keep it off. Why? They want instant gratification. Tons of people give up within the first couple of weeks due to minimal "results." Others go on extreme caloric-restricted diets to cut a ton of weight quickly, but then gain it right back by resuming their old habits shortly after. Losing weight, like anything we desire to do in our lives, is about the habits we adopt. We don't have to do it all at once, but we need to be consistent and intentional with our daily actions in order to form the habits that lead to positive change.

Darren Hardy's book titled, "The Compound Effect" discusses our daily habits (positive and negative ones) and the effects of those habits compounded over time. Hardy uses an analogy in his book to show the trap of instant gratification versus the compounding of positive daily habits. If someone were to walk up to you and give you the choice today to take $3 million in cash right out of their hand or take a penny that doubled in value for the next 30 days, which would you choose? In the heat of the moment, the easy answer for most would be to take the $3 million. As people, we naturally desire and want things immediately with little delay of gratification. On Day 10, that penny would only be valued at $5.12. On Day 20 it would still only equate to approximately $5,300 (a lot of money, but still nowhere near $3 million). However, by Day 30, the penny's value will have surpassed the three million dollars all the way to $5,368,709.12.

Can you imagine how would feel on the 30th day if you were offered that deal and you took the $3 million? Leaving almost $2.5 million on the table? Now you might be thinking, "Well, I'd still get three million dollars; life isn't too bad." I love the positive mental attitude, but the point isn't about the dollars, it's the concept. Too often we want things to come quickly; we want them to be easy and, often times, we take shortcuts to be instantaneously gratified. Real success lies in our consistency of action over time. We don't need to start with "all-in" large actions, but rather, consistently compound small positive actions to create long, sustaining change.

I use examples of "The Compound Effect" frequently with my basketball players. For example, 50 extra jump shots, five times a week, for 50 weeks would equate to 12,500 extra jump shots a year. After I walk through the math with the players, I ask them a few questions such as, "If you were to take 12,500 extra shots a year with great technique in a game-like setting, do you think that would make you a better shooter?" The kids all nod their heads yes. Yet, so many players are under the impression that they need to take 500 shots a day or spend an excessive amount of time to improve a skill. The same thing happens to many individuals when setting specific goals. They look at the big picture and think that they need to spend inordinate amounts of time or make drastic changes overnight to reach their desired goal. Instead, what they really need is a list of commitments over time that will help bridge the gap between where they are now and what they want to become.

Hardy also talks about "The Compound Effect" from a negative standpoint as well. For example, if I chose to have dessert after one meal it probably wouldn't kill me. Over time, however, if I make that same conscious decision I would unquestionably begin to see the negative effect on my physical performance along with gaining additional weight.

Another example would be if I were to skip a workout. No one is going to notice if I skip one workout. I may feel lower amounts of energy throughout my day, but more than likely I won't even notice. If I were to skip a week of workouts; however, I would certainly feel it and would probably start to notice it on my appearance. If I did this consistently over time, numerous other people would begin to notice as well. Whether it is a positive action or a negative action that we perform in our lives, our actions compound over time to shape the person we become. Jim Rohn, a now deceased author once said, "Success is a few simple disciplines practiced every day; while failure is simply a few errors in judgement, repeated every day."

LBTF:

- Delay the urge for instant gratification.
- We don't need to make transformations overnight. Start small and be consistent.
- Rather than focusing all of your attention on a list of goals, figure out who you want to become or what you want to accomplish. Then make a list of things that you are willing to commit to on a daily basis to get there.

CHAPTER 11: +1

When I attended Pewaukee High School in Wisconsin, Clay Iverson was the head varsity football coach at the school. I never played football in high school, but I often lifted weights in the mornings with the football team and attended a summer school class he instructed. Like the many of the athletes who played for him, I respected his style as a coach. He held athletes to high standards but did so in a way that made you want to run through a wall for him. Coach Iverson always got the most out of his teams and players.

Now in the coaching field, I always try to tap into people who experience continued success at any level. Coach Iverson, who is now the head football coach at a neighboring school in Wisconsin, started putting +1 at the end of several of his posts on Twitter. I sent him a message to find out what the meaning was. He proceeded to tell me, "+1 means doing a little bit more than the average person would every day in all aspects of life. I think when people think of greatness it is very abstract. This allows us to put meaning behind it. Are we doing a little extra every day? Those +1's add up to form our personal greatness. We even talk about brushing our teeth in a plus one fashion. We also talk about shortcuts; those add up as well to take away from how great we could be."

Like The "Compound Effect", +1 is about consistency in our positive actions. +1 is about doing a little more than what is expected and making the extra effort that other people may not be willing to make. It's about striving for our personal best through the development of great habits and the understanding that our actions play a large part in who we become as a person. If we consistently do a little extra, as Iverson said, we put commitments behind abstract goals or destinations.

Positive transformations in our lives don't happen overnight; in order to achieve something meaningful, it takes the building of positive habits that can be sustained through time. +1 is a great way to help remind us that putting a little extra effort in everything we do in our lives compounds over time to help mold us into the person we want to become.

A +1 Restaurant

The Crossings is a small mom-and-pop diner near my hometown of Pewaukee, Wisconsin. If you were to walk into the restaurant you wouldn't be blown away by flashy decorations or captivated by their dazzling menu. They open at 6 AM and close at 2 PM on a daily basis. They have a large menu, good food and reasonable prices. At first glance, you would probably consider it to be a normal restaurant. Unlike other restaurants, however, there are days when you can't get a seat during the lunch hour. Why? Their service.

The small staff of servers takes the time to not just write down your food order and bring it out to you, they take a keen interest in anyone who walks through the doors. They know numerous customers on a first-name basis. The manager, who is also a partial owner, makes a point of visiting tables and asking people how their experience was. If a customer doesn't have a good experience, she takes it personally and does whatever she can to remedy it. Food is always served in a timely manner, drinks are always full and tables are always clean regardless of how busy the place is.

Many restaurants will set out to make their mark by going above and beyond in their first few weeks, but when the initial excitement is gone they start to take shortcuts. They begin to think that just serving food is enough. While some of those places may find a way to remain in business, most will fail. In a study done by the Restaurant Brokers, it was estimated that up to 90% of restaurants that are independent establishments will go out of business within their first year. The Perry Group also did a study on upstart restaurants and agreed that most operations will close within their first year. They also added that 70% of those that make it past the first year will close in the next three to five years.

The Crossings has been in business for almost nine years. Many of their employees have been there for an extended amount of time. Several of their customers have been coming to eat since they opened. They've become a place where people want to enjoy their breakfast and lunch. How they've created this environment isn't complicated, but it requires making an extra effort and doing it on a consistent basis.

LBTF:

- Do a little more than the average person or the average business and do it consistently over time.
- Even the small things such as brushing your teeth or going out of your way to ask someone how their day is add up over time to create your personal greatness.

CHAPTER 12: THREE PILLARS

To get better at something you have to give full effort, in the right way and over an extended period of time. The three pillars to maximize improvement in anything we do are:

- Hard

- Smart

- Consistent

Many people understand what hard work is. We all would mostly agree it's giving maximum effort to a task. If we don't put effort into something, we aren't going to get much better at it. Hard work is our foundation for improvement. The other pillars; however, are equally important to maximize improvement. If we give maximum effort and we do it consistently, we are going to improve. If we give maximum effort while being smart and calculated with it, we are going to improve. In both cases, however, there is a cap on growth because of a missing pillar.

Two Runners

Take these scenarios as it relates to two different people trying to run their first 5K. Let's assume that both give maximum effort on each run.

Runner 1 runs six times a week. Throughout those six days, he does a variety of workouts but doesn't really have a plan and rarely calculates what he's doing. He drinks soda and eats pizza throughout the week, and never stretches or warms up. Runner 1 is generally concerned with getting his run in and calling it a day.

Runner 1 is running hard and doing it consistently, which will allow him to improve having never run before, but he will not reach his full potential without a plan, a proper diet, and an engagement in a warm-up and cool-down. Runner 1 is not working smart.

Runner 2 runs when she can. At times, it is four times a week, other times it is two times a week. When things are really busy at work, she may not get to her run at all during the week. When Runner 2 does go for a run, she calculates her distance, engages in a thorough warm-up beforehand, and a cool-down stretch afterward. Runner 2 is very conscious of her nutrition, but only on days when she runs.

Runner 2 has a plan, engages in a proper warm-up and recovery, eats well, but fails to do it on a consistent basis. Runner 2 is working hard and working smart, but is not doing it consistently.

Hypothetically speaking, if neither runner has ever run a race before, will each put themselves in a position to run a 5K? Obviously other factors could come into play, but generally speaking, I would say yes. Both runners, however, are limiting how well they could run their 5K due to a missing pillar of maximizing improvement. Some people work hard and do it consistently, but they don't do it smart. Others work hard and work smart, but they fail do it consistently. In both of those scenarios, the common denominator is that a lot of people do work hard or have the right intentions of hard work, but the disconnection is in the ability to do it smart or do it consistently.

Work Smart

I'll never forget during one of my first years in running my business, I sat up late one night doing my taxes in Microsoft Word (you may be thinking, "What an idiot," - that's fair). My roommate at the time asked what I was doing, and I replied, "Working on my taxes for the year." He looked over at me and said, "Work smarter, not harder, brother. That's about the dumbest way you could do it." I asked him to give me a better way. He insisted he could set up a spreadsheet in a few minutes that would make things much quicker, easier and more organized. I think I gave him $20; he set up a spreadsheet for me with formulas, and a tracking system for each category in my revenues and expenses. I still use a similar format almost five years later.

I had heard the phrase "work smarter, not harder" before, but, in that moment, it made more sense to me. In reality, it probably only saved me twenty to thirty minutes each week, and then two to three hours at the end of the year. The spreadsheet didn't dramatically change my life or my business but, as we have discussed, small amounts of time and efforts compound over time. I could potentially use those thirty minutes every week on something else, which ultimately adds up to 1,560 extra minutes over the course of a year. I would like to believe that if I had an extra 26 hours of time each year to focus on other aspects of my business that it would help me improve.

Time as a Measurement

Get in, get out, get better. An exercise center in Wisconsin has a motto that people can either work out with intensity or they can work out for a long time, but cannot do both. While this is vague and possesses a ton of variables dependent on the person and amount of time, the approach is right. It is similar to one of my favorite quotes, "It's not the number of hours you put in, it's what you put into the hours." From a personal perspective, I used to concern myself with the amount of time I put into everything. How many hours I was in the gym or how much time I spent studying. The validity of my efforts always came from how much time I put in.

We often think that because we have put in the time, results will come. Not necessarily. What we are putting into the time has a much greater effect on the results we will achieve. Are we focusing our time on the right things? Have we eliminated distractions? Do we do things consistently or only when it's convenient? We have to evaluate our work, training and pursuit of our dreams at a much higher level than how much time we put into things.

LBTF:

- The three pillars of enhancing a skill are: hard, smart and consistent.
- The blend of all three pillars allows for maximal improvement.
- Time is not always an accurate assessment of our efforts. Instead, we must ask ourselves if we are maximizing our time spent.

CHAPTER 13: PRODUCTIVITY

One of the toughest things for anyone to do is give an honest critique of their self. Many people have a clouded vision of their productivity. Two phrases I hear frequently are "I'm staying busy" and "I don't have any time." John Wooden is famous for the quote, "Don't mistake activity with achievement." When players tell me they don't have time to get into the gym or tell me they are always super busy, it tells me they aren't truly serious about their development. If something is important enough to you, you will MAKE the time to do it. I would also argue that most people who think they are busy are actually quite inefficient with their time.

I dare any person reading this to track their lives in 30-minute blocks for the next week. It's amazing what we will come to find. What we thought we were doing and what we thought we were accomplishing each day is nowhere near what we are actually doing and what we are actually accomplishing. One thing that is 100% equal in each person's day is that we all have 86,400 seconds of time. Are you truly maximizing your 86,400 seconds? Only you know the answer to that question. Track and evaluate your time. What needs to be cut out to allow more time on the important aspects of your life? In the next pages, we will discuss strategies to create more productivity. If we were to find just thirty more minutes each day for a whole year, we would have 182.5 hours at the end of the year that we could potentially direct toward something meaningful in our lives.

Multi-Tasking

If you are like me, you might think that doing multiple things at once should allow you to be able to get more accomplished, therefore allowing more time in your day. In all actuality, it is the exact opposite. Multiple research studies have proven that individuals cannot effectively focus their mind on more than one task at a time. The more we try to do at one time, the less likely we are to accomplish what we set forth to do, therefore extending the time it takes to complete that task. A Harvard Business Review study in 2010 found that multi-tasking leads to as much as a 40% decrease in productivity and increase in stress. Other studies have shown that it takes 50% longer to accomplish a task when multi-tasking. Essentially, most people that multi-task are really just going from task to task and are performing each one with less productivity than if they were to do one at a time.

A way to break the habit of multi-tasking is to put our important daily activities into separate groups. Within these specific groups, we then create blocks of time in our schedule and daily routines where we solely focus on that particular task. I like to describe this activity as time chunking. When I take the time at the beginning of my day or the night before to chunk my time and organize my tasks, I find myself drastically more efficient for the day. Too many times in the past, I found myself sitting down to prepare workout layouts and diagrams for the upcoming week and two hours later I look at the sheet of paper and have a quarter of my task accomplished. I would get caught into the trap of reading an email that came up onto my screen, which then led to me reading an article, responding to a text message and getting completely off task.

Instead, I now try to begin my day by allocating time chunks for important tasks in my day such as reading, writing, workout preparation, scheduling, responding to emails and returning phone calls. When I set out to work on a particular chunk that is my sole focus for that period of time.

Some days my chunks of times are larger than others, but organizing my day into blocks of activity helps me stay on task much more than jumping task to task throughout a day. Instead of checking my email and reading three articles, I now check my email and save articles I want to read at a later date so that I can respond to emails and move on. I read those articles in a different chunk of time. When I sit down to do workout preps, my phone is in another room. I also use pen and paper to not allow myself to use my computer to search something on the internet or respond to an email. I still fall victim to the desire of trying to accomplish multiple things at once, but time chunking has greatly helped to alleviate distractions and increased my overall productivity in a day.

Examples of Time Chunks for Me

- Exercise
- Workout & Practice Preparations
- Email Responses
- Reading
- Scheduling
- Phone Calls

What are three to five things that you need to accomplish in your day? Write those out with an allocated amount of time that you will spend focusing solely on that task. It is important to map out and properly organize your time in order to maximize it. By time chunking, we create a layout of tasks that we want to accomplish and avoid the distractions that can delay us from completing them.

Procrastination

Procrastination coincides with multi-tasking as both involve taking our attention away from the primary task at hand. Procrastination is defined as the delay or postponement of a task. For most people, procrastinating is caused by not wanting to do something; it is an attempt to delay the inevitable. Many of us fall victim to procrastination in some part of our lives, whether it be a responsibility at work, home or our personal lives. Kids procrastinate on their school assignments and household responsibilities. Adults procrastinate on projects at work or exercising. They wait until the last possible minute to do something (or don't do it all) by finding other things unrelated to the task to fill their time. Often, people who procrastinate many times are the same people who are stressed, overwhelmed, and feel as if they never have time for anything.

Our attempt at delaying a task actually detracts from our time to do other important tasks in our lives because our attention shifts to things that often serve no value or are simply a waste of time. If we would exercise personal discipline in our lives on things that we don't always want to do, we would, in turn, create more time and opportunity to allocate time to things that we did want to do. To conquer the negative habit of procrastination, we have to be willing to accept discipline into our lives.

Sometimes We Have to Say "No"

Saying "no" to certain things will allow more time for us to say "yes" to the things we deem most important in our lives. For everything we say "yes" to, we are saying "no" to something else. We have to align our answers of "yes" and "no" with the priorities we have in our lives. If you are unhappy with your weight, it would be in your best interest to say "no" to dessert at the restaurant and "yes" to your friend who asks you to engage in a workout routine with them.

Sometimes we feel obligated when people ask us to join them for certain things, so out of an obligatory feeling we commit to something that isn't important in our lives at the time. These are the instances in which we must learn to say no. There is absolutely a time and a place for fun, enjoyment, and a great time, but we also must align our actions with our aspirations. I used to have friends constantly calling to go out on the weekends, but I knew every time I would say "yes" to them, I am saying "no" to commitments I can be making to other places in my life. Do I go out with friends sometimes? Absolutely. I also know, however, that sometimes I have to say "no" in order to keep certain priorities at the forefront of my life.

I have heard numerous successful people say that if you have more than three priorities in your life, you really don't have any priorities. To identify your priorities, you must first know who you want to become. Then it is up to you to make the conscious decision of taking action on what truly deserves your time. As for the activities outside of your priorities, you'll need to learn that sometimes you just might have to say "no".

Habit Stacking

I got the idea of habit stacking from James Clear in his book, "Transform Your Habits". Habit stacking consists of taking an activity that is already engrained into your daily routine (showering, brushing your teeth, driving in a car, etc.) and engaging in a positive habit along with it. Some examples might be:

- When stopping at a red light while driving, you say one person you are grateful for in your life.
- While driving, instead of listening to music, listen to a podcast or interview with someone you admire.
- While eating a meal, you read 5 to 10 pages out of a book.
- While showering, you repeat a daily affirmation ten times. (Examples: I am healthy and strong or I am a grateful person regardless of my circumstances.)
- Before brushing your teeth at night, you reflect on the best moment of your day.
- While at work, you do ten pushups and ten squats every hour. You do the same while watching television.

Every morning while eating my breakfast, I listen to a podcast or a motivational video. In addition, I always write out three things I am grateful for in my life. I read for five to ten minutes before I brush my teeth each evening. I do not brush my teeth until I have read something informational. Every morning, I know I am going to eat breakfast, and, every night, I know I am going to brush my teeth. Stacking positive daily habits with those things has made a significant impact in the way I start and finish each day. By stacking beneficial habits with other productive habits that we already perform, we maximize time while increasing the positive behaviors in our lives.

LBTF:

- "I don't have time" simply means that something is not a priority. If something is truly important in our lives, we make time to do it.
- Multi-tasking and procrastination are poor time-wasting habits that dampen our productivity levels and in turn leave us feeling stressed or overwhelmed with the responsibilities in our lives.
- Time chunking is a great way to alleviate multi-tasking and procrastination.
- Habit stacking is a strategy we can use to promote further positive behaviors in our lives without using inordinate amounts of time.

CHAPTER 14: GARBAGE IN, GARBAGE OUT

I know people who have the news on all day as background noise, others who watch it in the morning and the evening. I know kids who are on YouTube for hours at a time looking up videos of people doing absolutely ridiculous things. I also know that if I search YouTube and look up, "people doing stupid things" there are thousands of videos with millions and millions of views. On the flip side, if I look up a successful author giving a keynote presentation or sharing fundamentals to their success, I get multiple videos with only thousands of views in comparison to the millions on people doing stupid things. If we feed our minds garbage, we will produce garbage. No different than the mind, what we feed our bodies is what we get out of our bodies. If we constantly feed our bodies pizza, fast food and ice cream, we will produce low amounts of unsustainable energy and add multiple pounds of unnecessary weight. If someone wants to be fat, feel bloated, and have low amounts of energy, I am in no position to tell them differently. They should keep going through the drive-thru every night ordering an extra-large soda, and devouring ice cream for dessert at every meal.

I want to make it clear that we should watch funny videos and enjoy television shows or movies. We should enjoy a beverage or dessert from time to time. What I also want to make clear is that if those are the activities you partake in on a consistent basis, I don't want to hear complaints about money problems, being overweight or being at a stagnant point in your career. If garbage is constantly going in, garbage is going to constantly come out.

Maybe we want more happiness in our life or to get better at our job; maybe we want to start a business or just become smarter. It all starts with our actions. We need to stop watching the news and start reading books. Instead of spending hours on YouTube looking up people doing stupid things, we should find people whom we admire or look up to and learn how they reached the level they are at. Maybe we want to be lean and toned. If that's the case, there has to be a sense of pride in what we fuel our body with each day. It's not a complicated process, but it takes a level of personal discipline that many don't have. It's why there are also many out there that have a glaring gap on where they are currently and where they want to be. Garbage in, garbage out.

The Power of Reading

During the summer months when we were kids, my sister and I would come strolling down the stairs to a list of items we were to accomplish before our parents got home from work that evening. When those tasks were done, we were free to enjoy our summer days. The lists would always consist of simple tasks such as do the dishes, vacuum the house, and then at the end it ALWAYS had "read for 20 to 30 minutes." I dreaded seeing that on the list. The last thing I wanted to do was read during the summer. I wanted to get on my bike and ride to the basketball court as quickly as possible. More times than not, I flipped the pages of a magazine and then left it out somewhere thinking it would give the impression that I did my reading for the day. Sometimes I just flat out didn't do it. My parents were smarter than what I probably gave them credit for, and looking back I have an inkling that they probably knew that's what I did. They didn't ask for a book report, or a summary of what I read, they were just trying to encourage and instill in me the habit of reading.

I certainly didn't understand the power of the habit then, but I absolutely do now. The amount of information that is shared through books and articles is endless. Many of the most successful human beings in the world share their strategies, stories and accounts of what allowed them to get where they are today. I have read so many powerful, mindset-changing books that I wish I would have read when I was younger.

I now spend a minimum of two hours per week (typically more) reading. Most people who don't read will typically say they don't have the time to read when the fact of the matter is that they aren't willing to MAKE the time to read. I know plenty of people who spend two hours alone on Facebook, Instagram and Twitter every day. Can you imagine what we could become if we spent that time (even half of that time) tapping into the strategies of some of the most successful people in the world?

The bridge between who we are in the present moment and who we want to become can be shortened in an extremely short period of time by making the commitment to self-improvement each day. There are going to be numerous days where we don't feel like reading, or we would rather surf the web and watch funny videos, but I challenge you to read something informational for 20 to 30 minutes each day and see what you become in the process. The author Jim Rohn once said, "Formal education will make you a living, self-education will make you a fortune."

Yoga

Like many others, I perceived yoga as "just stretching" and even stereotyped it as something only females do. I go to yoga classes each week and am the only male 95% of the time. I have learned that not only can the workout itself be challenging for anyone, but the practice of mindfulness is beneficial for anyone. I certainly enjoy the physical component of the class, but for me, the value of each class comes in the practice of mindfulness. Being mindful means that we are engaged and focused on the present moment. When focused on the present moment, we have the ability to operate from a place of clarity rather than a place of obligation or stress. Oftentimes we run ourselves ragged trying to keep up with our obligations on top of trying to keep everyone else in our lives happy. We become consumed with prior events or future responsibilities clouding our ability to operate at our best in the present moment. I know that when I feel overwhelmed or stressed I lose patience, which has a direct effect on my ability to relay information in a manner that is most beneficial to my athletes. Not only are my athletes affected, but other people close to me in my life are affected as well. I become short-tempered and allow things that shouldn't bother me to bother me. Stress in one area of our lives has a tendency to spill over into other areas of our lives unless we have the ability to redirect our focus and gain control of it. Research has proven that people cannot feel stressed and blessed at the same time.

The instructor of the yoga class that I attend regularly once said, "We all are given a certain number of breaths; by slowing down our breaths, we add longevity to our lives." In other words, we slow our lives down by slowing our breaths down. Whenever I feel my responsibilities are piling up and stress is increasing in my life, I stop and try to redirect my focus to breathing which helps put me back into the present moment, and on things that are within my control. Engaging in the practice of mindfulness, we learn to redirect our focus onto our breath and ultimately let go of the things we cannot control. As with anything, the practice of mindfulness is not something we can do once or twice and become experts. I frequently attend yoga classes to focus my thoughts and practice deep breathing. In doing so, I have learned how to slow down my mind, leading to increased productivity and performance in other areas of my life.

LBTF:

- What we fuel our minds and bodies with is what our minds and bodies will produce. Feed your mind with positive information; feed your body with quality nutrients and exercise.
- There may not be a more powerful tool in bridging the gap to where we are today and where we want to go than developing the habit of reading.
- I included 20 books in the back of this book from which I have greatly benefited. I believe that anyone reading this would also find significant value in those books as well.

CHAPTER 15: REST

In college, as an exercise science major, we obviously were taught a great deal about the principles that relate to exercise training. Two principles that we talked about frequently were those of adaptation and reversibility.

Adaptation

When the body engages in physical exercise, or in other words, when it is physically stressed, it goes through a process of breaking down and then rebuilding the muscles used. If the body is stressed within reasonable limits over time, the function of those muscles improve; the body positively adapts to the stress that was placed on it. If, however, the body is overstressed and not allowed time to adapt and recover, overtraining and injury can occur. When we put in the proper time, energy, and commitment towards our aspirations, we too can continue to grow and improve our own function over time. Too much time, energy, or constant stressing of our mind and body, however, can cause us to over train and burn out.

Reversibility

The principle of reversibility states that if a muscle isn't stressed or used sufficiently over time, it will atrophy. In other words, use it or lose it! When we become complacent in our lives and do not continue to grow and improve ourselves, we spiral backwards. The key is finding the optimal load of time and energy to put forth in each section of our lives in order to maximize personal growth.

Overtraining

Overtraining is something to which many athletes fall victim to. It typically results from working really hard and consistently, but not very smart. I had a player ask me to review his weight training program prior to basketball season. He said he was working out often but not seeing or feeling any results. I told him to write out day by day what he was doing, how much sleep he was getting and what he was eating. I wanted to see everything. After looking it over for a couple of minutes, I came to an easy conclusion -- he needed rest!

So often we engrain ourselves with a mindset that more is always better, when in all actuality less is actually better in some cases. This was a prime example. This particular player had a program that consisted of five strenuous days in which he was completing several sets of about eight to ten exercises each day. Many were compound exercises, which involve multiple joints and usually involve higher stress that he repeated multiple times during the week. He wasn't allowing his body any time to recover. I suggested he take a full week off from the weight room and see how he felt.

Approximately four days later, he sent me a text message that stated he already felt a difference. By the time that week was over, he told me he felt a dramatic difference. The message? In order to get the best results in our lives, we not only need to give maximum effort, but also allow ourselves time to recover. Schedule downtime into your week. Take vacations. Take time in your day where you shut off your phone or your email. We all need time to rest and recover. Constantly running yourself thin will only cause burn out, added stress and lower quality of work and life.

Enjoy the View

A friend of mine has a different way of wording it, but subscribes to a similar principle. He says, "There is no sense in getting to the top if you don't enjoy the view." So often we get caught up in our day-to-day commitments such that we forget to enjoy each day. We forget to relish in the simple pleasures or the parts of our lives that we have earned due to our commitments and sacrifices.

This is a battle that I constantly fight. I have earned the ability to be able to take vacations every once in a while. Often times while on that vacation, however, I am in constant battle with my mind that I should be doing more or something "productive". In time, I have learned to slow my mind down and "enjoy the view". Why put in all the work if we don't enjoy the fruits of our labor? I have also learned to schedule downtime in my life. I try to watch a movie every couple of weeks, go out to dinner with a friend once a week and watch at least one television show each week. It doesn't sound like much, but it helps me to refresh my mind. I also try to take some sort of vacation every three to four months and get away for an extended period. I will typically allow myself an hour each day to stay caught up on emails or other tasks, but the remaining portion of the time I'm away, I attempt to actually be away. When I am able to do this, it never ceases to amaze me how much more motivated I am to get back to my normal routine and lifestyle. I almost always come back more productive and efficient than I was previously.

LBTF:

- Our minds and bodies need time to recover in order to maximize our full potential.
- Build time into your schedule to allow your mind and body to refresh and recover. Everyone is different, but maybe it's a TV show, dinner with a friend, workout class or sleeping in one day.
- Take time to enjoy the view. It will leave you feeling more gratified in the work you have done and be more motivated to continue your quest for personal excellence.

CHAPTER 16: SELF-REFLECTION

A former basketball coach of mine always used to say to us after games to "look inward" and reflect on the game we had just played. He wanted us to evaluate our play from a personal basis; what we did to help the team or what we could have done better to help the team. If someone was disgruntled with playing time, he wanted them to reflect on if what they had been doing warranted more playing time. He was engraining the tool of self-reflection in each of us. The problem that I had was that I didn't have a strategy that allowed me to properly and effectively reflect on my performance. Often times the basis of my reflection was focused on my stat line or the result of the game. I focused my attention on outcomes and not the process that led to those outcomes or how those results were created. Using outcomes as the basis to reflect on performance is a poor way to evaluate ourselves, our teams and organizations because outcomes are only partially within our control. Outcomes can also be vague and broad, as opposed to reflecting on specific moments and aspects that played a part in the outcome. Our time in reflection should be spent on specific elements of our performance as well as controllable items such as our attitude toward adversity and how much effort we put forth in our preparation.

Tale of Two Salesmen

Two employees working for the same company have the responsibility of selling fitness memberships for the various facilities across a 50-mile radius. They receive a commission based on the number of memberships they sell per month. At the time of their hiring, both employees were told by their boss that he recommends that they partake in self-reflection to help them in their jobs. The boss didn't give any specific instruction on how they should reflect, he just told them he recommended some reflection. Both salesmen were great employees and wanted to do right by their boss. Employee #2 read some books and was prepared and well-equipped on self-reflection. Employee #1 didn't put in much effort in self-reflecting and instead focused on outcomes. Employee #2 reflected on specific elements of his sales meetings and evaluating things within his control. They both wrote down their reflections and evaluations in their notebooks.

Employee #1

- 6 new memberships
- Total months sold: 18
- 2 members signed up for personal training
- Sold the most memberships of any salesperson
- Total commission made in two weeks: $250

Employee #2

- The best moment of my week was making such a strong connection with a customer that she asked me what I suggested for membership options. Take-away: Keep working on building connections with customers rather than pushing sales immediately.

- The worst moment of my week was when I told a customer the wrong prices on our individual membership plans. Take-away: Either carry the prices with me or better familiarize myself with them.

This is a fictitious example, but one that paints the picture of the difference between reflecting on controllable items and outcomes. In so many organizations, executives, managers and employees are driven by numbers and outcomes. They run reports only on their numbers at the end of each quarter. They judge their success solely on those reports. Results are important, I get it, but focusing your attention only on results rather than the process of achieving those results is detrimental to an organization as well as an individual's long-term success.

Jeff Bezos, the CEO of Amazon, says, "If we have a good quarter, it's because of work we did three, four or five years ago. It's not because we did a good job this quarter." What Bezos is saying is that in the short-term, numbers-driven reflection may make sense as a measure of success, but it doesn't tell the whole story. Individuals and organizations also need to focus on the process.

When we focus on the process we turn our attention not to outcomes, but the learning and growth through both positive and negative moments. Here are a few questions you can ask yourself as an individual or use in an organization to help employees better evaluate their performance.

- What was the best moment of your day/week? What made that the best moment?
- What was the most difficult decision you made this week? What did you learn from that challenge?
- What are specific things you are excelling in right now? Why?
- What areas need more work? What can you do to continue to grow in the areas that need more work?

- What was your mindset like after a mistake or challenge?
- What things in your control did you excel at today?
- Was there a time when you shifted your focus to uncontrollable rather than controllable actions?

Strategies for Self-Reflection

Self-reflection can be a great tool in helping us identify our struggles and how to overcome them. It can also be used as a tool to guide us in identifying the things that are going well in our lives and help continue to encourage those behaviors. Here are four other strategies you can use to self-reflect.

1.) What Went Well Journal

If there was one strategy of self-reflection I wish I would have used earlier in my life, it would be a "What Went Well Journal". If you search "What Went Well Journal" on Google you will get a multitude of different ideas on how to put one together. The basis behind the idea is that you are reflecting on what went well within a particular event, day or even week. The key is consistency. We remember things the more we think about them. We also are able to recall things better when we write them down. A "What Went Well Journal" is a way for you to not only reflect, but also train your brain to recreate the best moments of a particular event, day, or week. To complete a "What Went Well Journal," get out a pen and paper. Take an event that you participated in and write 15 to 20 things that went well from that event. Then write three areas for continued growth. At the end, write a brief summary on your take-away points from that event.

2.) Watch Film

Film is an extremely powerful way of teaching as it allows us vivid images of ourselves in action. Although it is most frequently used in the sports realm, it is not just for athletes and coaches. Just about anyone can benefit from watching and analyzing film on themselves. I love the idea of having individual and team highlight reels. Seeing positive or memorable splices of ourselves can create images of success, which helps our mind recreate those moments prior to an event. From my own experiences of watching film, there is also great benefit of watching things we have done wrong to make corrective actions. Many times we don't realize a mistake that we are making until we see it. I frequently use film to help players of all ages and ability get visuals on things they are doing well along with things they need to improve upon. Last year for one of the youth basketball teams I coach, my assistant and I devised a strategy aimed at helping our players to see things through a coach's lens. We asked each of them to be the coach for a given period of time. They were to stop the video and point out teaching moments for the individuals as well as the team. As the season progressed, we often referenced and issued reminders from the film study. As a result, the players better understood certain concepts due to seeing the clips.

3.) Ask Others for Feedback

Talk to a coach, teammate or colleague. Ask for positives in your performance as well as areas for growth. Write them down. Reflect on the comments they made and devise ways to continue expanding on the positives, as well create strategies to continue to learn, grow, and improve on the other aspects. Keep in mind to make sure you are listening to the right people. Seek people who tell you what you need to hear, not what you want to hear. Seek others who came before you and have succeeded in a similar position.

4.) Ask Yourself Tough Questions

I ran across a great example of this strategy by Mike Procopio, a basketball player development coach for the Dallas Mavericks. It was posted on the blog of his website, www.hoopconsultants.com. Procopio spoke about how many players are often disgruntled with their role or aren't seeing the results that they desire. He formulated a list of eleven questions that a dissatisfied player should ask themselves.

Have I...

- Put in extra work with coaches before/and or after practice?
- Put up 200 to 300 jump shots a day to perfect my craft on my own?
- Done strength and conditioning workouts consistently to make sure that my conditioning is at its best?
- Watched film on games and asked a coach to critique?
- Watched film on upcoming opponents to make sure that I was prepared for them?
- Sacrificed staying up late and going out in order to ensure I get 8 hours of rest?
- Showed energy in practice and made an impact to stand out to coaches?
- Not been on time, but 20 minutes early, to all team required functions (i.e., practices, meetings and film sessions)?
- Honestly outplayed the players above me in the rotation in practice and in workouts?
- Done anything on or off the court to get my coaches upset?
- Met with coaches and asked what I need to do to get on the floor more?

Write out tough questions you have for yourself. Openly and honestly evaluate each one. Don't focus solely on results or outcomes, focus on specific elements that effect those outcomes. Evaluate if you are truly working hard, smart and consistently.

LBTF:

- Self-reflection is a way to evaluate progress and identify areas for improvement.
- Reflect on items that are within your control; focusing solely on outcomes can be a misleading measure of actual performance.
- Focus not just on negatives or areas for growth; find things that went well. In doing so, we encourage ourselves to continue that behavior.

Foundation 3
INFLUENCE

Who are examples of great leaders? I often ask this question to young athletes when I am conducting a basketball clinic. The answers I receive range from the names of historical figures and great athletes to the names of people in their family. I ask the kids what makes someone a great leader, the responses are usually something like this:

"He's the best player."

"She's in charge."

"They make their teammates better."

"He sets a good example."

"She's the captain."

The last thing I do is ask the kids to raise their hand if they think they are a leader. Some hands go up, some stay down. Usually the best players in the gym or kids that have been captains previously are the ones who raise their hands. The kids who don't raise their hands think they aren't leaders because they have never been given a title that makes them feel like one.

The same thing can happen in any role of our lives. We devalue the influence we have due to not feeling like we possess a particular role that is deemed important based on a title. I proceed to tell the kids that they, like all of us in any role, have the power to be leaders. In its simplest form, leadership is influence. This is not to say that there aren't people in certain positions who have more ability to positively or negatively influence than others. What this is saying, is that no matter the role each of us possess, there is power to influence. If everyone has the power to influence, they then have the ability to lead in some capacity. The actions an individual takes and the way they treat others determines the type of influence they have. LBTF is about creating positive influence in every role of your life. This section will outline the qualities that each of us can tap into to positively influence.

CHAPTER 17: OUR INTERACTIONS MATTER

I was running a basketball clinic for a group of 6th to 8th grade girls who were all at various levels of ability. Some were very good and needed some guidance, while others needed a significant amount of work. One of the girls was clearly new to the game and required extra instruction, a situation that occurs frequently. I often relay some encouraging words of wisdom to these players along the lines of, "Mistakes are part of the learning process. We won't improve by doing things that do not challenge us." She looked at me and shook her head. That was a regular encounter; that's what most kids do. Throughout the session I gave her bits of feedback in certain instances and she continued to do her best. It wasn't until a couple of sessions later that she came up to me and said, "Hey Coach Taylor, I just wanted to say thank you. I usually come to camps and I always get nervous and never have fun; this was the best camp I have ever been to." Nothing I did was out of the ordinary, but this encounter made me realize how important each interaction is that I have with every player. We never know when something we say or do will have a lasting impact on someone else.

Many reading this in the United States probably have never heard the name Sean Fitzpatrick. Fitzpatrick was the most successful captain of the most successful rugby team of all time. Like many kids in New Zealand, his dream was to always play for the All Blacks rugby team. By his own account, Fitzpatrick wasn't sure he would ever reach that mark. He is quoted as saying, "I was a little fat kid, I dreamed of playing for the All Blacks but I never thought I'd play for them."

Fitzpatrick attended secondary school (grades 7 to 13 in New Zealand) at Sacred Heart where they had 15 rugby fields, and a 16th field for baseball, hockey, football, cricket, and on occasion another rugby field. On Fitzpatrick's first day of rugby, instead of walking onto the first field or even one of the other top fourteen fields, Fitzpatrick walked to the 16th field and was greeted by Guy Davies, who would be Fitzpatrick's coach. Davies was an accounting instructor with limited rugby knowledge and low fluency in the English language. Fitzpatrick says on the first day of practice Davies said three things that changed his life. "First thing, everyone on this team is equal, from me right through, everyone is equal. Second thing, all I want when you turn up at field number 16, is to turn up with a big attitude. Thirdly all I want is for you individually to be as successful as you can be. Be as successful as you can be." Fitzpatrick believes that encounter and that advice was a motivating factor for him moving his way up from the 16th team at Sacred Heart to become not only a captain, but the most successful captain in All Blacks history. I can guarantee that in this situation Davies didn't have any intention of inspiring a young kid into having one of the greatest rugby careers in the history of the sport.

I will never forget an old basketball coach of mine looking at me as I was shaking, trembling, and about to give up while doing a challenging exercise in practice. She looked me straight in the eyes and said, "Sometimes you gotta be a little bit crazy. Sometimes you gotta push past your limits." To this day she has no idea those words still resonate in my head. I don't have any contact with her, but I can still picture her face, hear her tone and visualize the environment I was in when she said that to me. I don't know why it struck a chord with me, but I wrote the words, "Sometimes you have to be a little crazy" on a piece of notebook paper and hung it on the door of my room when I was in high school. When I woke up some mornings and didn't feel like getting up or when I was in the midst of a difficult workout, I would tell myself those exact words. Those words had a big impact in molding me as a person. I constantly try to push past my limits, and sometimes I do have to do things that other people view as "crazy". That single encounter was a huge moment in my life. It helped me start to break down mental barriers and drove me to not settle for where I was, but continue to push myself onto new heights. Our interactions matter!

Pay It Forward

As I was driving to work one morning, I decided to make a quick stop at Starbucks. Rarely do I stop at a drive-thru, but that morning I was low on food in my house and craved a coffee. I ordered two breakfast sandwiches and a large coffee. As I pulled up to pay, the lady behind the window looked at me and said, "You're all good." I paused and thought "Wow, I must have gotten a great night of sleep last night." I asked if she was sure. She proceeded to tell me that the person in front of me in the drive-thru picked up my bill. I quickly realized it had nothing to do with my hairstyle or looks that day, it was the kindness of the person in front of me. I asked if that was common, and she said that the person who did it for me often paid for the orders of the next people in line at the drive-thru. She also said there have been other occurrences like this at other Starbucks locations. I was shocked; I never heard of anyone doing this before. After thinking about it for a couple of seconds, I picked up the bill of the person behind me. I have no clue how long this went on for, but the simple act of kindness by the person in front of me created a domino effect that made we want to do the same for another person.

When I got home that day, I went online and looked up if this was indeed a regular occurrence at Starbucks. It turns out it was and is. A chain was once started at a drive-thru in Florida that went eleven hours and 378 customers long. Whether you are a supporter of Starbucks or not, that is pretty cool. It shows the power of what a random act of kindness can do. The person who picked up my bill was being intentional about making someone else's day. I wanted to do the same. Positive energy and actions are contagious. These actions don't have to involve money or any resources. Making someone's day better can start with a smile, a compliment or something as simple as opening a door for someone who has their hands full.

LBTF:

- Our interactions matter. We never know when something we say or do will have an influence in somebody's life.
- Random acts of kindness are contagious.
- We all have the ability to influence in either a positive or negative manner through our actions.

CHAPTER 18: MODEL

Mahatma Gandhi wasn't famously quoted for saying "Talk about the change you want to see in the world," he was quoted as saying, "Be the change you want to see in the world." He didn't just speak to thousands of people about a nonviolent disobedience movement, he was at the front and center of it. The words he spoke wouldn't resonate to whom he spoke to until his actions proved worthy. Gandhi became one of the most talked about and storied civil rights activists the world has ever seen. His words certainly had an impact on people, but it was the actions he modeled that influenced others to follow his lead.

John Wooden, the former legendary coach for the UCLA Men's Basketball program once said, "Young people need models, not critics." Wooden's statement is correct in not only young people, but all people. One of the easiest things to do is criticize, complain, and talk about what we wish to see in others. The question to ask ourselves first is, "Are we modeling the behavior we wish to see?" Words are shallow if we don't support them with actions. How can we expect someone to treat us with respect if we don't treat others with respect? How can we expect someone to do extra work on their own time if we too do not do the same? How can we expect someone to demonstrate great body language if we have poor body language? As it relates to the younger generation, parents pass along much more than their genes to their children. They pass along the habits, actions and behaviors that they demonstrate within their home environment. Well-mannered kids usually have well-mannered parents. In my time coaching, I've learned that kids aren't always listening to what you say, but they are always watching and observing what you do. It's often the same in any venue. Actions speak a lot louder than words. Before we can hope to see a behavior in someone else, we must first model that behavior ourselves.

Setting a Poor Example

A group of boys that I get to coach were in Kansas City to play in a large, showcase-style tournament in which numerous teams from various parts of the country would be attending. In our division there was a program financially assisted by a well-known, successful NBA player. It just so happened that this particular player was traveling with the teams that his program sent to the tournament. There were six courts at the venue each being full with college coaches, parents and players from other teams. Most people in the gym recognized who he was. In previous games he sat on the bench with his groups and would act as an assistant coach. He was mild-mannered. In our game however, that changed quickly. We were in control of the game early in the first half with a lead of about six to eight points. A call was made by a referee in our favor that I'll admit was a questionable call, but in our own defense, there had been a few calls in the half that were questionable going the other way as well. The NBA player erupted. He stood up and challenged the referee in a demonstrative fashion, where he received a quick technical foul (keep in mind he is at the end of the bench and not the head coach). The referee asked him to take a seat and not say anything else. The man did the exact opposite as he got more angry and started approaching the referee leading to another technical foul. Two technical fouls led to his ejection from the game. Rather than leave the gym and do some damage control on the lesson he was setting for his players, he decided to get face-to-face with the referee, and while I didn't witness it, some say there was physical confrontation. The other coaches on the team didn't stop there either, they picked up technical fouls as well. As tournament directors and other officials broke up the chaos, the NBA player and his other coaches grabbed their kids and took them off the floor. They quit the game with three minutes left in the first half. To top it off, the next morning the team was back. I spoke to the coaches very briefly in passing and the only thing I could smell was alcohol on their breath.

Here you have a guy sponsoring a program, and in principle doing something positive for his hometown community, yet setting an extremely poor example. The amount of influence that this professional athlete has on these kids is likely very high; he has the ability to influence their lives in a positive or a negative manner. Whether he believed the referees were doing a good job or not, what he modeled to his players was that when it isn't going your way, quit, complain and make an absolute fool out of yourself. From what I hear, this player does not typically behave this way, but when you have the status and influence that this person does, lots of people are watching, and the example he set not only for those on his team, but for other players and teams in the gym was poor.

A True Role Model

My father is one of the hardest working people I know. When you talk about success not being an accident, he exemplifies that. When I was young, I would roll out of my bed, walk down the stairs and more often times than not, my dad was already at work. When I got home from practice later in the evening, he'd just be getting home or when times were very busy, he might even still be working. I remember when my mom, sister, and I would drive to his office and bring him dinner on some nights. I certainly didn't understand the efforts he put forth when I was young, but he worked as hard as he did to make a better life for everyone else. My sister and I were both lucky enough to have the opportunity to go to college and leave debt-free because of his and my mother's efforts. I think today he would probably agree he overdid it at times and put a lot of pressure on himself to grow and run a successful business. No matter how much he had on his plate, he never missed a game of my high school basketball career nor did he miss a home college game. Even if it meant he had to spend extra time on his work that evening or get up earlier the next day, he still kept family as his priority. He wanted to be there to support us while giving us endless opportunities in our lives. When I look back, I don't ever recall my father pleading, begging or lecturing me to work harder. He didn't have to. The example he set each day was more powerful than any words he could've spoken. He taught me the value of work ethic and sacrifice through his actions, not his words.

LBTF:

- The words we speak don't resonate with others until our actions prove worthy.

- Before we can hope to see a behavior in someone else, we must first model that behavior ourselves.
- It's important to remember that we are always being observed, what actions we are modeling?

CHAPTER 19: SERVICE

The 12th and final step in Alcoholics Anonymous is to become a mentor. Why does this matter? It matters because we can't truly become the best version of ourselves until we help someone else become their best. So in other words, it is important to strive to be your own personal best (the first 11 steps of AA), but at the end of the day we can't become our absolute best until we help others become their best. Service is about being a part of or engaging in something bigger than yourself. For Alcoholics Anonymous, service is about helping someone else overcome their addiction. For others, it might be volunteering at a local charity, coaching, teaching or something as simple as making dinner for your family. If you feel like your life lacks purpose or meaning, you have the ability to change that by beginning to serve. We all have the capability to be a part of something bigger than ourselves. Jon Gordon, the author of many New York Times bestselling books, says that we don't have to be great to serve, but in order to be great we have to serve. When we help others we not only add value to their lives, but we also enrich our own lives.

Sacrifice

Service involves sacrifice. Sacrifice can be defined as the act of giving something that is valued for the sake of something else that is regarded as more important or worthy. Husbands and wives sacrifice money, time and freedoms in their lives in order to have a child and start a family. Many great athletes have sacrificed going to clubs and parties to reach the highest level in their sport. There are numerous examples that all of us can probably think of off the top of our heads. For me, my parents are the best example of service and sacrifice. They constantly gave up pleasures in their life and sacrificed so much time and energy to make not only my life, but also my sister's life better. Helping us with homework, driving us place to place and working extra hours so that we wouldn't have to worry about if we were going to be able to go to college; the list is endless. I also think of the coaches in my basketball career who spent significant time after practice to help me improve when they could have been at home resting or relaxing. I had teachers who stayed after school to help me understand a subject. We all have people in our lives who have sacrificed their personal pleasures to help serve our needs. They invested in us and poured their hearts and souls into helping us become who we are. Those people exemplify what Leave Better Than Found is all about.

I don't think I can talk about or think of service and sacrifice without mentioning the men and women who make up our military. We could argue the various reasons to join the military, but in most cases those who enlist desire to be a part of something bigger than themselves. They want to serve our country and the people in it. Members of the military sacrifice family time, income and social lives so that the United States of America can remain a free country.

In 2002, I was in eighth grade, and was a huge sports fan. In my scope of the world not much else could be more important than being a professional athlete. Pat Tillman, who at the time was a NFL safety for the Arizona Cardinals, turned down a three-year, 3.6 million dollar contract to enlist and serve in the army. For those of you who don't know Tillman's story, he was later shot and killed in Afghanistan in 2004. Tillman was quoted in 2002 as saying, "Sports embodied many of the qualities I deem meaningful, however these last few years, and especially after recent events, I've come to appreciate just how shallow and insignificant my role is." Before starting his military service, Tillman married his high school girlfriend. When this news hit the press and was discussed on ESPN (the only channel I grew up watching), I really didn't understand it all. In my amateur mind I could only think of how this guy had the life. He was a pro athlete about to make millions of dollars, why would he risk all of that to enter into the military? In Tillman's eyes he had a bigger calling, he desired to be a part of a cause bigger than himself. He wanted to serve. He sacrificed his NFL career and ultimately his life to do so. There are not many better examples of service than Pat Tillman and the entire military. A heart-felt thank you to anyone who has served and is currently serving in the United States Military; thank you for helping protect the freedoms that we are all fortunate to have each and every day as a byproduct of living in this country. No amount of gratitude will ever be enough to thank you for your service and sacrifice.

You don't have to be famous, rich or blessed with immaculate talent to serve. You don't have to enlist in the military, become a parent, coach or teacher either. When we have a desire to be a part of something bigger than ourselves and are willing to sacrifice time, energy or any other personal resource we have for a cause, we positively influence the lives of others, and enrich our own lives in the process.

LBTF:

- We can find peace, significance and meaning in our life when we serve.
- As best-selling author Jon Gordon says, "We don't have to be great to serve, but in order to be great we have to serve."
- Change your mindset from, "What do I get?" to "What can I give?" Find ways to be of service to your family, friends, colleagues, and community.

CHAPTER 20: HUMILITY

I look back on a debate that a friend and I once had regarding confidence and cockiness. As with most debates and opinion-based arguments, there was probably some type of middle ground to the discussion. We argued back and forth on athletes who portrayed confidence as opposed to cockiness. I don't remember exactly how the argument finished or what we drew as a conclusion, but looking back, I can now draw a conclusion that I believe both of us would agree on. The fine line that separates confidence from cockiness is humility. It's having an ego but not allowing it to turn to conceit. Ego is a person's sense of self-esteem or self-importance. We all have an ego. Most successful people in fact have a high ego; they view themselves as important and believe they possess inherent value to the world. There's nothing wrong with having a high ego, unless it turns to conceit. Conceit is an excessive ego in which a person looks down on others, and believes their value to be above that of their peers. The middle ground again comes back to humility, which is derived from the word humble. To be humble is to have a modest opinion of one's importance. It's the belief that we have value and possess strengths, but never at the expense of others. We all have room to grow and improve regardless of our status. Confidence and cockiness. Ego and conceit. In the middle lies humility.

Entitlement

A person who feels entitled often believes that he or she is deserving of a special right or privilege. Many times their belief stems from a place of conceit. They feel as if they should be given something that most others should not because of who they perceive themselves to be. The All Blacks New Zealand Rugby Team guards closely against entitlement in their team culture. "Sweep the Shed" is a mantra they use within their team to signify that regardless of ability or rank, no player will ever be too big to do the small things. After each game the All Blacks play, the players are responsible to clean the locker room. Whereas most professional teams have a janitorial staff and multiple equipment managers to clean up, the All Blacks have their own players do it. They use this as a staple of their culture. The organization wants its players to understand that it is a privilege to wear the All Blacks jersey, and in order to keep that privilege, each player must perform certain responsibilities, one of which is cleaning the shed after the games. While some may consider this a far-fetched strategy, it certainly makes it clear that no one within their team is entitled to anything; everything is earned.

My mother and father protected my sister and me from growing up with an entitled mindset, they often said, "It's a privilege to be a part of this family and to live in this home." When I heard this phrase it typically meant I had just been assigned to perform a chore that I had absolutely no desire of doing. My sister and I grew up in a household where we had little financial concern. We never worried about where our next meal came from or about wearing the same clothes every day. We were definitely fortunate to be raised where we were. It would have been easy for both of us to take for granted the privileges we had or to act in an entitled manner believing that we deserved these things. My parents raised us in a way that didn't allow us to do so. We had to maintain a certain grade point average, perform chores and act in a respectful manner. Saying "please" and "thank you" were mandatory in our household. If we didn't do our part or follow the rules, there were consequences. If we wanted something, they never handed it to us, we had to work for it. They made sure we were given opportunities in our childhood, but made equally sure we earned them. We understood just as quickly as an opportunity could be given, it could be taken away. From an individual perspective, we must never begin to believe that the world owes us something. We are owed nothing. When we operate from a place of humility instead of entitlement, we learn to appreciate the privileges granted to us rather than expect them.

"Get Off the Court"

During a practice my freshmen year of college I made a mistake, and out of frustration I yelled at a teammate. I'll never forget the moment that ensued after and the lesson I learned. Coach immediately blew the whistle when he heard me attempt to deflect my error onto someone else. He lit into me in front of the rest of the team, and I deserved it. "You're going to blame that on him? You want to be a point guard at this level? A leader? That's embarrassing. Take some responsibility," he said. As we were just about to start play again, he looked at me with an angry face and shouted a phrase that rung in my head, "Get off the court." As I walked off the floor, I knew I messed up. Coach taught me a valuable lesson that day to own up to my mistakes. So many times in our lives pride gets in the way of our mistakes; we don't want to admit that we are wrong. We think that in admitting our mistake we are weak. As I found out that day, the real weakness lies in the person who thinks they have never made a mistake. The first person I went and talked to after practice was my teammate who I tried to blame for my mistake. I apologized for my actions and assured him that I would be better in the future. Humility is having the courage to admit when we are wrong, then follow it up with action to amend our mistake.

Learn from the Best

I received a text message after the first week of the HBO Series "Hard Knocks: Training Camp with the Houston Texans". It read,

> *"A lot of talk on sports radio today if JJ's work ethic is real or if it is for the cameras. Thoughts?"*

JJ Watt is a friend of mine and one of the best players in the NFL. The person who sent me this message certainly may have been trying to stir some emotion out of me, but it's not the first time I have ever been asked that. Do people really think a guy who went from being a two-star recruit in high school to a two-time NFL defensive player of the year just works hard for the cameras? Or might there be more to his success? The reason why he has been able to accomplish what he has is because of the work ethic and habits he created before cameras were ever around. There have been several articles, features, and interviews highlighting his unbelievable work ethic, but the part that still baffles me is that people would rather search for flaws in his greatness instead of figuring out exactly what he has done to reach the level he is at.

Being around JJ often, I can tell you that he is constantly learning. He is a great example of someone who is always looking for ways to improve. One way he does this is by tapping into the minds of other successful people. When he meets someone at the top of their profession, he doesn't assume they got where they are because they are "naturally talented' or they "got lucky." Instead, he asks them questions about their success. What do they know that he doesn't? What did they have to do reach the pinnacle of their profession? How do they handle fame, fortune, and success? JJ knows the person at the top of the mountain didn't fall there. He is constantly learning and never stagnant. This is a guy who signed a $100 million contract, yet he is always looking for an edge and a way to get better. What if we all started tapping into this power of curiosity? What if our thought process became, "What can I learn from them?" instead of searching for flaws and making critiques?

Wisdom is Everywhere

While tapping into the best, most successful minds in our world is a great tool for learning, we can look anywhere and find wisdom bestowed upon us. Let's take dogs for instance. Dogs always find great joy in the small things. Fetching a tennis ball, going for a walk, riding in the car and being served a meal are things that literally make my dogs jump for joy. Dogs are loyal, selfless and demonstrate unwavering enthusiasm on a daily basis. We can also look at young kids and gain significant wisdom. They often remind us of certain qualities such as curiosity and risk-taking. Kids are always exploring, examining, and figuring things out. They are willing risk-takers and rarely think about "playing it safe". They aren't afraid to ask questions and have a constant desire to learn. Am I telling you that you should act like a dog or a child? No. I am telling you that there is wisdom everywhere around us; the more we seek, the more we find.

LBTF:

- Everyone has an ego. When our ego turns to conceit, however, is when we no longer have humility.

- We all will make errors and mistakes in our lives; own up to and learn from them.

- No matter where we are, what level we have reached, there is always room to grow.

- Wisdom is everywhere, the more we seek it, the more we find it.

CHAPTER 21: APPRECIATION

Most of us have probably performed a job that we probably received low pay and at times, low appreciation. For me, I was a bag room employee at a country club for a few summers. There were awesome people who appreciated the work that you performed for them, equally, there were people who were jerks. One of our tasks in the bag room was to clean the member's clubs and store them after they had just got done golfing. We had a small garage located below the clubhouse where the members would leave their clubs for cleaning and storage. Some of the members would come into the garage and leave us generous tips, some would simply look you in the eye and tell you that they appreciated your efforts. Others would drop their clubs, make demands, and treat you as if you were their personal servant. They would complain about a small patch of grass on their pitching wedge that wasn't cleaned the time before or that their bag was not perfectly placed on their cart 45 minutes before arrival. Those same people were the ones who never could muster a please or thank you. They were energy takers.

I don't say so proudly, but I can admit that I took shortcuts during my time working at the country club. I often worked until close which usually meant whatever time all the clubs were cleaned, and our other responsibilities were taken care of, we could leave. I can tell you with certainty that I didn't lose any sleep cleaning three out of the ten clubs of someone who constantly complained and never showed any type of appreciation toward us. Some of the other guys working were even worse, they would just go store the clubs without even thinking about cleaning them. I can also tell you with certainty that regardless of what time it was getting to be in the evening, I, as well as other employees, always gave extra effort to those people who made an effort to show appreciation towards the work we did for them. We remember how those people made us feel, they gave us energy and pride in a job that could get very monotonous. It didn't mean that they had to leave us a large tip, it simply meant that they were aware enough to just say two simple words and mean them. I can think of three or four members to this day who never left a tip, but always said a sincere thank you. I always made an extra effort for those members. Thank you's or some form of appreciation can go a long way. The opposite also holds true as well. When people only hear complaints or feel as though they are being scolded all the time, they will eventually find ways to take shortcuts. Temporarily, the people who complain and make demands may get what they are looking for, but at the end of the day, no one is going to go the extra mile for them if they don't feel appreciated.

Kevin Durant

The MVP of the 2013-2014 NBA season gave a moving speech after he was presented with the prestigious award, and that speech still hasn't left my memory. Durant was filled with humility as he credited the numerous people in his life that helped him reach that point. He told a personal tale about every single one of his teammates and how each one contributed to him winning the MVP. He passed out sincere and specific praise to his coaching staff as well as members within the organization. As Durant came to the end of his speech, he told stories about his childhood where his mother sacrificed nights of eating to make sure that her kids could eat instead. He credited her for keeping his fire lit even when he wanted to give up. As his emotions turned to tears, he called her the "Real MVP." His words clearly came from the heart. It would have been easy for Durant to talk about everything he had done to get to that point, but he opted to credit others in his life instead. He understood that no one reaches the level he has on their own; many people played a significant role in his success. Durant obviously had a large role in becoming the NBA MVP, but he clearly comes from a humble beginning in which he was shown the value of appreciation.

LBTF:

- People want to feel valued. When we show signs of appreciation toward our colleagues, family members or players they are much more likely to go the extra mile for us.
- Appreciation also goes a long way in receiving better service.
- We all have had some help along the way; recognize those who have helped you get to where you are today.

CHAPTER 22: CARE

Many would argue that she doesn't really have a choice. She married the guy and has been with him for nearly sixty years, it's not like she's going to leave him now. My grandma often jokes and says this to people when asked how she puts up with my grandpa. The real reason "she puts up with him" is because of how much she cares about him. She models this in her actions on a daily basis. Besides pouring Cheerios and milk into a bowl, I would be hard pressed to find a time when I witnessed my grandpa cooking a meal for himself. The same can be said about doing his own dishes.

When my grandpa had his legs amputated it was easy to see how much life would change for him and the struggles that he would soon ensue. It was harder to remember that my grandma's life would also change. Just like my grandpa, she didn't flinch. Whatever difficulties were ahead, she planned to be there like she always had been. When my grandpa was released from the hospital, I will never forget how many times a personal nurse was suggested for him. Neither of them ever thought twice about it. I remember my grandpa saying, "I have a nurse," and then pointed at my grandma. Anything you can think of from showering, getting dressed, using the bathroom, providing a ride, making a meal or getting something from another room that he wanted, she would do and do so with undivided attention. Rarely do I hear my grandparents profess their undying love to each other, but you realize very quickly after being around them why they have been together nearly sixty years. A large part of the reason is because of how much they care about each other.

My Sister

Another note I received before I started chemotherapy was from my sister. It was short and simple but a reminder to me that she cared.

> *"Here's my little reminder to you that I believe in you and your incredible mindset to overcome any obstacle. Know that I am always here and will support you however I can. I will be your visitor whenever you need or want anything, or your personal assistant when you just don't want to get off the couch."*

My sister and I don't often have elaborate conversations or talk on a daily basis but we have always understood each other. She is two years younger than me and one of the most caring and supportive people in my life. I always know that if I need something from her she almost always willingly drops everything to help. The note she wrote me is a perfect depiction of how she cares. When we were younger, she never missed any of my basketball games despite having plenty of opportunities to do other things. I had my fair share of struggles during my career, but she knew I wasn't the type that wanted to constantly discuss them. Her presence and unconditional support was what I needed, and she always gave it.

As we have grown older, I ask her for rides to and from the airport, to cook a meal, watch my house or help me with graphic design for my business. She never hesitates and always makes time to help. None of those actions seem like much, but they make my life easier and despite the inconvenience it may have on her, she is always willing to do it. It doesn't matter when the last time we've talked or what I ask her to do, her care is unconditional. While I probably should remind her more, I am incredibly thankful to have her as a sister. One of the main reasons being that she truly cares about me and my well-being.

A Special Bond

If you were to listen in on a conversation between myself and a small group of my closest buddies, at times you would probably think we were anything but friends. All of us pass out and receive verbal shots from each other. When we argue it is often about senseless topics that probably won't be important shortly after the conversation is over. When it's all said and done however, we have an undying loyalty that stems from how much we care for each other. There have been many moments in our young lives where we have counted on one another. When I had cancer, I could always rely on this group of friends to "keep it real" with me. They made jokes about me one minute, but were there to bring me food and support me the next minute. I'll never forget a moment before starting chemotherapy when the four of us were in Mexico. As many of you know, in several types of chemotherapy, hair loss is a common side effect. We made the decision to shave the hair off my head together before I lost it during treatment. As my buddies took a razor to my head we shared a flurry of emotions. I felt a special connection to each of them in that moment. No matter what any of us had, were, or eventually were going to go through, we each had each other's back and genuinely cared for one another.

LBTF:

- Care stems from having a genuine concern or interest in another person.
- We can show we care in a variety of ways; the strongest way to show we care is through our actions.

CHAPTER 23: LISTEN

Listening is an active engagement in what the other person has to say within a conversation. There is eye contact, active questioning, and genuine interest in the other person. Hearing is being present, but not being fully engaged or interested in what the other person has to say. Listening and hearing are not the same action.

What seems like such a small gesture, listening can go a long way in creating sustainable relationships in both our personal and professional lives. We show people they are valued through appreciation as well as showing a genuine interest in who they are. Listening builds connections. The better we connect with and understand others, the stronger our relationship with them becomes. Stronger relationships create empathy, understanding and trust. When we take the time to engage others and not just hear what they're saying, but actually listen, it is amazing the information we come to find, and the relationships that we can create.

Everyone is Connected to Iowa

At some point while listening to my grandpa tell a story there is always a part of me that is thinking his next words are, "Crazy thing about it, he's from Iowa too." I'm exaggerating a bit, but it seems that he always finds a way to tie his stories back to his home state of Iowa. He makes connections to his own life by listening and taking a genuine interest in other people. It doesn't matter who the person or what the situation is, he takes time to find something in common and then build a connection. He has a special way of making someone feel important; there is always something in their life that he finds fascinating. Oftentimes we approach conversations halfheartedly, meaning that we ask people a question out of courtesy or because we have been engrained that it's the right thing to do, but how many of us take the time to listen to the response and actively respond? How many of us try to find a connection with that person?

My grandpa started a business in 1975. He is now retired, but still has relationships with people from his first years of business. My father has been a business owner and still is currently. The common theme that I have discovered is that their success isn't due to their intelligence (it helps, they are both extremely smart), it's due to how they connect with others. They both built successful businesses based on people, not on numbers. It's not a hard concept, but so often in a conversation we get wrapped up in ourselves and all of the responsibilities we are faced with, that we forget to take a genuine interest in the other person's life. We forget that they, like us, are important and have a story too. Take the time to get to know someone and actively engage in conversation. Who knows, they might be from Iowa too.

LBTF:

- Listening and hearing are not one in the same, listening is an active engagement in a conversation.
- Take a genuine interest in someone else. Ask about their background, day, weekend, family, upcoming events and hobbies. Asking questions shows you have a genuine interest in the other person.

CHAPTER 24: EMPATHY

"But I already told you my whole life story, not just based on my description, cause where you see it from where you're sitting it's probably 110% different, I guess we would have to walk a mile in each other's shoes at least. What size you wear? I wear tens. Let's see if you can fit your feet."

-Eminem, lyrics from song, Beautiful

Whether or not you are a fan of hip-hop artist, Eminem, many of his songs contain lyrics with lessons that offer value to anyone willing to listen. In this song, "Beautiful", his message is that each of us possess unique personalities, different backgrounds and experiences. It's safe to say that everyone has judgements and at times follow preconceived notions regarding other people. It's easy to get caught in the trap of shunning a person due to preconceptions rather than taking the time to get to know them or "walk a mile in their shoes." Practicing empathy allows us the ability to deepen connections with others. I want to be clear in stating that we will run across people we don't like, who take advantage of us or have poor values. We won't get along with everyone, but having empathy is the restraint of preconceived judgement. Oftentimes we jump to conclusions faster than we should. We don't examine an entire situation or get to know someone on a deeper level to make our own judgement.

Empathy also allows us to look past our narrow scope of perception and see the world from the lens of someone else. When I coach young players, empathy is crucial for me in relaying an effective message. One of the most common mistakes (I can say it because I've fallen victim to it numerous times) that occurs in coaching (and in leadership, teaching, parenting, etc.) is that a coach sees something in his head that is simple, but in the minds of those who he is teaching it is complex and confusing. The kids don't know, understand, or see the same things the coach does. Rather than examining a different way to teach, giving another reminder or using a different visual demonstration, the coach becomes frustrated and yells at the kids for not performing the task correctly. As I discussed previously, there are times when the players may be at fault, maybe they aren't listening or following the directions, but I have discovered that more often times than not if each kid is struggling, the blame is on the coach, not the player. Rather than jumping to the immediate conclusion that the kids are not listening or following directions, it's important that the coach digs deeper and "walks a mile in their shoes".

A different example could be a typically strong employee who is now underperforming because of family problems. The easy solution for most managers would be to scream and scold that person while the tougher solution would be to figure out what has caused the decline in performance and offer support. Now again, if the employee is making poor choices or simply underperforming because they no longer care or value their job, then it may be time to cut ties, but we must resist jumping to conclusions until we have identified the root of the problem.

A leader is often synonymous with boss, coach, captain or manager. A difference however, is that a leader understands his or her counterparts, they have built a connection with them. They have walked a mile in their shoes. We must take the time and energy to see the world from not just our lens, but others around us. When we only see things through our own lens, we often times miss out on opportunities to serve and help bring out the best in other people.

LBTF:

- Empathy is the ability to walk a mile in someone else's shoes.
- Ignore preconceived notions and form your opinions and judgements.
- Look outside your scope of perception and see what the other person might be seeing from their lens.

CHAPTER 25: LOVE

On our last days will we have to run around and make up for love we didn't give or talk about regrets we have? How will we be remembered by our family, friends and peers? When I think about my Grandma Sue, who passed away a few years ago, the first thing that comes to my mind is her non-stop joy. The moment any of my family members walked into a room with her, you knew that meant more to her than anything else in the world. From a financial standpoint, my grandma was not rich by any means, but what she didn't have in wealth, she multiplied in terms of love. She always wanted hugs and she never missed a chance to tell you how much she cared about you. She could see things in people that they didn't even realize themselves. "Taylor, someday you're going to be a teacher," she would tell me and I would reply, "No chance," with an attitude and grouchiness of a typical teenage kid. "You might not know it now, but you will be," she would say in a calm, confident voice. Grandma, if you're reading this where you are, you were right. My job description may not say school teacher, but my passion and life are centered on the opportunities to teach and help young people. Grandma knew best.

I'll never forget the latter portion of her life as she battled cancer and underwent multiple serious surgeries. I was home for spring break from college and my mom was going to check on and visit my grandma like she regularly did. I wanted to go with her to see my grandma. My mom wasn't sure if she wanted me to go initially, as my grandma's memory and actions were being affected heavily by the strong medications she was on. My mom was looking out for me. She didn't want that to be the lasting memory I had of my grandma. I knew my mom had my best interests in mind, but there was nothing that could have changed my memories of my grandma, who she was to me and how she positively affected the lives of others. When it came Grandma's time, everyone she valued in her life knew how she loved them unconditionally. While it's never easy to lose someone you care about in your life, I can confidently say that my grandma left us with no regrets and endless love for others that will always be felt by her closest family and friends.

LBTF:

- "People may forget the words you said to them, but they will never forget the way you made them feel." –Maya Angelou
- Value those closest to you in your life and never miss an opportunity to show you love them.
- How do you want your closest family and friends to remember you?

CHAPTER 26: INSPIRE

Jim Valvano, a former NCAA Division 1 Men's Basketball coach, and Stuart Scott, a former ESPN SportsCenter anchor are both names in which anyone who follows sports have probably heard of. Even if you aren't heavily into sports, there is a chance you may have heard these names. What do they both have in common? Unfortunately, they both lost their lives to cancer, but in the process, helped transform millions of other lives. In Stuart Scott's 2014 speech at the ESPY Award Show, he talks about the V Foundation, a charity started by Jim Valvano dedicated to cancer research. Scott talks about the impact it has had on those fighting cancer all over the world and the inspiration and hope that Valvano was able to give people just like him. Scott's speech inspired and moved people in the same way that Valvano's famous 1993 ESPY speech did. Shortly after Scott's speech he passed away, which prompted a buzz all over news outlets and social media about his legacy and what he meant to so many people. During his memorable speech he said, "You beat cancer by how you live, while you live, and in the manner in which you live. Live. And fight like hell." Those words, just as Valvano's famous words from 1993, "Don't give up, don't ever give up," will live on in the hearts of many forever.

I urge anyone reading this book to pull up a computer, and watch each of these ESPY Award Show speeches from 1993 and 2014. They are incredibly powerful, moving, and will cause you to immediately remember what is important in our lives. In each of their speeches, they talk about how grateful they are for the incredible blessings they have. They talk about the people most important to them, and how they hope to leave a legacy in which inspires others. These are both men speaking in front of thousands who had been given only months left to live. We don't need to be sick to take inspiration from these two. Spend time with people you love, be thankful for all the beautiful things in your life and attack each day with unwavering enthusiasm. In the process, you will leave a legacy that inspires others to do the same!

"17 Minutes of Pain for a Lifetime of Memories"

That was the quote that ran through my head much of that cold, fall Saturday morning my junior year in high school. My buddy Kyle isn't known for being an outspoken guy or being powerful with his words, but undoubtedly he is a passionate individual. During my junior year of high school, I was a member of a very good cross country team. At the sectional meet, we needed to finish in the top two out of the sixteen team field to advance to state. This was no easy task. Three of the top ten teams in the state for our division were in our sectional (us being one).

The night before that meet, Kyle wrote an individual note to myself and the six other runners on our eight-man team. Each note was hand-written and about a page long. The notes all had a personal twist with the same quote at the bottom of the page. He talked about our friendship, our struggles, and the love he had for each one of us. He was the only senior on our team, and from a time perspective, he was our best runner too. In all likelihood, he would have made it to state as an individual either way, but going to team state was something he and all of us were striving for. As I read his note I could feel every word coming out of the page; it came from his heart. Each guy understood how much going to state as a team meant to him, and none of us wanted to let him down.

That next morning, our team ran better than we had all year, setting numerous personal records that allowed us to clinch a birth into the 2005 Wisconsin State Meet. While I always put forth maximum effort and had a strong level of success in running, I definitely didn't get super fired up to run 3.1 miles and have my legs, chest and arms burning the whole time. After reading this note however, I was fired up. I was inspired to perform at my highest level.

Today, that note still hangs in my bedroom. The quote at the bottom of the note reads "17 minutes of pain for a lifetime of memories". There are a lot of memories from that experience I will never forget. One of those memories being the note that Kyle wrote and how inspired we all were on that particular day because of it.

LBTF:

- We leave our legacy on the world in the manner in which we live each day of our lives.

- Inspiration can come in a multitude of different forms and is one of the most powerful things we can pass to others.

CONCLUSION

LBTF is an acronym to remind us of the value each of us has in each moment of our lives. Each of those moments add up to form our personal legacy. It doesn't matter who you are, what you have done, haven't done or where you are going, you have the ability to LBTF. Each foundational element of LBTF is within your control, regardless of your circumstances. We all have the ability to adopt a positive mental attitude, take action toward our aspirations, and spread positive influence. By tapping into the power of each foundation, we transform not only our own lives, but all those who surround us as well. We may not be able to change the world in its entirety, but we can entirely change our world and impact the lives of those in it. One day when we look back on our lives, we want to know we made the most of our time. We want to know that our time on earth made the world a better place. Don't wait until tomorrow to do everything you are capable of today. Your life matters. You matter. Take action now. Leave Better Than Found.

LBTF ACTION PLAN

1.) Clarify your vision. Who are you? Who do you want to become? Figure out what is most important in your life, who is most important in your life, and how you want to be remembered. Write it down. Place it somewhere that you will frequently see it.

2.) Shift your focus from goals to commitments.

- What do you want to become great at or improve upon?
- Make a commitment list of things you are willing to do each day. What daily actions will it take for you to get better?
- Start taking small, consistent action every day.
- Delay gratification. Think about "The Compound Effect".
- There is no greater goal than being in pursuit of your personal best.

3.) Start a gratitude journal. Each morning write three to five things that you are especially grateful for.

4.) Be intentional with your words. Change "have to" to "get to." Come from a place of gratitude with your words.

5.) Pick someone in your life that you are especially grateful for and write that person a handwritten letter. The letter should include specific and sincere reasons you are grateful for that person.

6.) Read a book or watch a video of someone who you admire or think highly of. Take notes on key points and specific items or strategies that are applicable to your life.

7.) Identify a big event that was significant in your life recently. Create a "What Went Well Journal" for it. If you haven't had any big events recently, do one on your entire last week.

8.) Start habit stacking.

- Identify something you would like to engage in more (i.e., reading, using daily affirmations, exercising, etc.).
- Find another habit in your daily life in which you already do each day (i.e., showering, brushing your teeth).
- Perform the desired behavior simultaneously or in conjunction with the habit that is already a staple in your day.

9.) Use time chunking to better organize your day and increase productivity. Map out the important activities in your day and reserve blocks of time to solely focus on the completion of those tasks.

10.) Donate-serve. This doesn't have to be money-related. A donation of your time,   energy and effort as a volunteer for an organization can give you a great sense of fulfillment and add significant value to your life.

11.) Show a specific and sincere form of appreciation for someone who has helped you. Saying "thank you" as you're walking away doesn't count. Look them in the eyes and tell them "thank you" or even better, specifically tell the person how they were able to help you and that you appreciate their time and service.

12.) Ask a person specific and sincere questions about their life. Take time to listen and learn about them. The questions don't need to be complicated, but asking people questions and making them feel important in conversation can build relationships. Here are some examples of questions:

- How are you?
- What's been the best part of your day so far?
- Where are you from?
- What's your passion?

- Best destination you've ever traveled to?
- Best part about your job?

13.) Remind those closest to you how you feel about them. Don't miss an opportunity to tell someone you love them.

14.) Remember that our interactions matter. Engage in random acts of kindness. Do something for someone else that you may never see anything in return for. Each moment of your life shapes the legacy you leave.

15.) Help us. Send us things you are doing or have done that relate to Leave Better Than Found. Whether you helped make someone's day or created something that will change the lives of millions, we want to hear how you did it. Follow us on Twitter, like us on Facebook, and share with us on our website.

BOOK LIST

I discussed the power of reading in this book. The list of books below is a short list of titles that I have read and found great value in. Committing to being a lifelong learner is a commitment to always seeking your personal best. If you are looking for more books outside of these titles or specific areas of focus, I would be happy to give further recommendations.

An Impractical Guide to Becoming a Transformational Leader, by Joshua Medcalf and Jamie Gilbert

Burn Your Goals, by Joshua Medcalf and Jamie Gilbert

Inside Out Coaching, by Joe Ehrmann

Legacy, by James Kerr

Life is Good, by Bert and John Jacobs

Relentless, by Tim Grover

Rousey, by Ronda Rousey

Start with Why, by Simon Sinek

Tell My Sons, by Lt. Col. Mark Weber

The Carpenter, by Jon Gordon

The Compound Effect, by Darren Hardy

The Energy Bus, by Jon Gordon

The Hard Hart, by Jon Gordon

The No Complaining Rule, by Jon Gordon

The Secret to Success, by Eric Thomas

The Seed, by Jon Gordon

The Talent Code, by Daniel Coyle

The Way of the Peaceful Warrior, by Dan Millman

Toughness, by Jay Bilas

You Win in the Locker Room First, by Jon Gordon and Mike Smith

REFERENCES

1. Atchley, P. (2010). You can't multitask, so stop trying. *Harvard Business Review*. Retrieved from https://hbr.org/2010/12/you-cant-multi-task-so-stop-tr/

2. Fredrickson, B., Coffey, K. A., Pek, J., & Finkel, S. M. (2008). Open hearts build lives: Positive emotions, induced through loving-kindness meditation, build consequential personal resources. *Journal of Personality and Social Psychology 95*(5): 1045-1062. DOI: 10.1037/a0013262

3. Firozi, Paulina. 378 people 'pay it forward' at Starbucks. *USA Today Network*. Retrieved from http://www.usatoday.com/story/news/nation-now/2014/08/21/378-people-pay-it-forward-at-fla-starbucks/14380109/

4. Ma, L., Li, Y., & Feng, M. (2015). Positive emotion and cardiovascular disease in elderly people. *International Journal of Clinical and Experimental Medicine, 8*(5), 6682-6686

5. Scheier, M. F. & Carver, C. S. (1993). On the power of positive thinking: The benefits of being optimistic. *Current Directions in Psychological Science, 2*(1), 26–30. Retrieved from http://www.jstor.org/stable/20182190

6. Wickford, H. (n.d.) The average life span of a restaurant. Retrieved from http://yourbusiness.azcentral.com/average-life-span-restaurant-6024.html

7. The Winning Zone. (2009). *Captain Fantastic Fitzpatrick* (30th ed.). Edinburgh: Scotland. Retrieved from http://www.inthewinningzone.com/wz/Magazine/June-2009/Captain-Fantastic-Fitzpatrick-/449/

ABOUT THE AUTHOR

Passion, energy and work ethic are common words that come to mind when people talk about Taylor Jannsen. Many of his current players, former teammates and coaches state that the passion and energy he brings to an environment is second to none. Immediately following his collegiate basketball career in 2011, Taylor founded PerformanceMax Basketball Training, LLC where he has had the opportunity to teach, mentor and serve thousands of young athletes across the country ranging from 3rd grade to the NCAA Division 1 level. Throughout his playing as well as coaching experiences, Taylor has gained infinite wisdom in motivation, discipline, handling adversity and building organizational culture. In the early part of 2015, he was given perspective that he perhaps wouldn't have found elsewhere at the current stage of his life. He was diagnosed with testicular cancer and would undergo chemotherapy treatments. Taylor recalls this time period as one in which he began to realize the influence he was having on others. It was during this time that he also began to formulate ideas to author this book, Leave Better Than Found. Today, Taylor not only brings his story, perspective and passion to the court, but also to any corporation, organization, team or individual looking to transform themselves.

SERVICES

Leave Better Than Found LLC

Taylor travels to perform keynote presentations for your corporation, organization and team across a broad range of industries and occupations. He brings an intensity and perspective to each presentation that is able to engage and inspire the audience. The content he covers challenges each person in attendance to pursue their own personal excellence while positively impacting the lives of others.

To book Taylor or connect with him on social media:
Website: www.leavebetterthanfound.com
Email: tjannsen@leavebetterthanfound.com
Twitter: @LBTFLLC
Facebook: Leave Better Than Found LLC

PerformanceMax Basketball Training LLC

The coaches at PerformanceMax Basketball Training, LLC go to great lengths to see that every individual becomes a better version of themselves on and off the basketball court. Each event is designed to challenge players and help unlock potential they never knew they had. Taylor has worked with thousands of players across the country ranging from youth to NCAA Division 1 level athletes.

For more information on Taylor's basketball training services or to book a camp or clinic in your area:
Website: www.pmaxbasketball.com
Email: performancemaxllc@gmail.com
Twitter: @Tjannsen

Made in the USA
Middletown, DE
22 February 2016